hopes and fears

hopes and fears

Trump, Clinton, the voters and the future

Michael A. Ashcroft

Biteback Publishing

First published in Great Britain in 2017 by
Biteback Publishing Ltd
Westminster Tower
3 Albert Embankment
London SE1 7SP

ISBN 978-1-78590-211-6

10 9 8 7 6 5 4 3 2 1

A CIP catalogue record for this book is available from the British Library.

Set in Adobe Garamond Pro

Printed and bound in Great Britain by
CPI Group (UK) Ltd, Croydon CR0 4YY

Contents

About the author

LORD ASHCROFT KCMG PC is an international businessman, author, philanthropist and pollster. He has many, varied business interests with significant investments and participation in both public and private companies in the United Kingdom, United States and the Caribbean. From 2005 to 2010 he was Deputy Chairman of the Conservative Party in the UK, having earlier been its Treasurer from 1998 to 2001. In September 2012 he was made the UK Government's Special Representative for Veterans' Transition, working with all departments to ensure military personnel receive the support they need when making the transition to civilian life.

His political works include *Smell The Coffee: A Wake-Up Call For The Conservative Party*; *Minority Verdict*; *Pay Me Forty Quid And I'll Tell You: The 2015 Election Through The Eyes Of The Voters*; *Call Me Dave: The Unauthorised Biography of David Cameron* (with Isabel Oakeshott); and *Well, You Did Ask: Why The UK Voted To Leave The EU*. He is also the author of *Dirty Politics, Dirty Times* about his battle with New Labour and *The Times* newspaper.

He is Founder and Chairman of the Board of Crimestoppers, the only UK charity dedicated to solving crimes, a Trustee of the Imperial War Museum, Chairman of the Trustees of Ashcroft Technology Academy in south London, Chancellor of Anglia Ruskin University, Treasurer of the International Democrat Union, a Trustee of the Cleveland Clinic and a Fellow of the Canadian Geographical Society.

Lord Ashcroft's life-long interest in bravery has led to him writing six books on the subject and building the largest collection of Victoria Crosses in the world. This collection is on display in the Lord Ashcroft Gallery at Imperial War Museum, London. The author royalties from each of his books on gallantry have been donated to military charities.

As part of his commitment to philanthropy, Lord Ashcroft has donated tens of millions of pounds to good causes in the UK and abroad. He has also signed up to The Giving Pledge, a commitment by the world's wealthiest individuals and families to dedicate the majority of their wealth to philanthropy.

His political research and commentary is published at LordAshcroftPolls.com. For more information about Lord Ashcroft visit LordAshcroft.com. You can also follow him on Twitter: @LordAshcroft.

Introduction:
the wisdom of the people

FOR THOSE OF US WHO HAD STAYED UP to watch the results trickle in from Britain's referendum on the European Union, there was something eerily familiar about the night of 8 November, 2016. For the second time in a year, the people had delivered a verdict that would surprise and horrify many in the political world and beyond.

For the previous two months, the Lord Ashcroft Polls team had travelled the United States to listen to the people who would decide whether to put Donald Trump or Hillary Clinton in the White House. In our focus groups, we spoke to partisans and – especially – undecided voters of all ages and backgrounds in seven swing states which turned out to be critical to the result: Wisconsin, North Carolina, Virginia, Pennsylvania, Arizona, Florida, and Ohio. I wrote week by week about what they had to say – indeed listeners to the *Ashcroft In America* podcast heard first hand, as well as my interviews with eminent participants in and observers of the American political scene such as Mitt Romney, Howard Dean, Rachel Maddow, Karl Rove, Joe Trippi and Jon Sopel.

Since I never make predictions about politics, it would be a bit much to claim now that we had any particular foresight of Donald Trump's victory. In any case, forecasting the result was not the purpose of the project. But looking back at the focus group findings, together with the results of a thirty-thousand sample poll we conducted over the final weeks, we can see how it happened.

I should make clear that I had no dog in this fight. As someone who has conducted political polling in the UK and Europe for over a decade, most recently focusing on the forces at play in the Brexit referendum, I was naturally drawn to such a fascinating contest. I came to observe, listen and learn, and to report what I found.

In this book I have brought together that research with two aims. First, I want to help understand how the result came about, because I think it can be, and in some quarters has been, misunderstood – particularly in Britain, where many have not grasped the appeal of Trump, or the widespread antipathy for his opponent. It is one thing to wish, as many do, that the voters had made a different decision. But it is quite another to say they must have decided as they did because they were duped or misled, or that they cast their vote out of ignorance or prejudice. I don't think that was the case at all. As we will see in the chapters describing how people saw the choice between Trump and Clinton, and on the parallels between the presidential election and Brexit, people approached the decision as electorates always do: as a choice between imperfect alternatives and uncertain futures. They had to weigh their desire for change against the risk that came with it. And seeing both candidates' failings, they had to judge which amounted to the bigger disqualification from office. Whatever you may think about the decision the voters made, they made it with their eyes open.

My second aim is to consider what the 2016 election tells us about the future. Our analysis of the various divisions in American society, together with the competing outlooks and agendas of the different kinds of voters who make up the new American electorate, reveals the scale of the challenge facing both parties. The Democrats' predicament is perhaps the most obvious. A common trait among losing parties that I have observed in my research over the years is the inclination to claim a moral victory. One manifestation of this tendency among Trump's opponents has been to point to the popular vote, which Clinton carried with a margin of nearly 2.9 million. But comforting though it may be, this fact is a distraction from the more important question for the party: why it lost supposedly solidly Democratic counties in states that had not voted for a Republican presidential nominee since Reagan. The temptation will be to say that voters who switched sides will soon realise what a terrible mistake they have made and come flooding back, but this only postpones the reckoning with the real reasons for defeat that must come before a party can return to office. Much will depend upon who has the upper hand in determining the party's direction – not least because, as our polling shows, the values and priorities of its activist core are at the other end of the spectrum from many of the voters it needs to re-enlist.

But the other side, too, has much to think about. The United States has never been so diverse demographically. At the same time, it hasn't been so politically monochrome since the 1920s. The GOP now controls the White House, the House of Representatives and the Senate (not to mention thirty-one of the fifty state governorships and thirty-two state legislatures). If this amounts to a stunning victory, it creates its own headaches: however little Trump has in common with his Republican colleagues, as far as the voters are concerned, with one party in charge there will be no excuse not to get things done. But what, exactly? There will be tensions to resolve, not just between the administration and Capitol Hill, but within the Republican voting coalition – between the cultural conservatives who constitute much of the party's base, and more moderate voters who worry most about healthcare and jobs.

Many look at the political scene, especially in America, and see plenty of reasons for despair: a more rancorous tone, increasingly bitter partisanship fuelled by a more fragmented and unforgiving media, readiness to believe the worst of opponents, and a terrible fate at the hands of his or her own supporters for any politician who dares work across the aisle. But I think our research also points to some reasons for hope. People recognise and regret the divisions before them. There is a desire to see problems solved. And while some worry about the outcome, others have had their faith in democracy restored. The electoral process propelled to the forefront a candidate who gave voice to people's frustrations, and put him in the White House. Many who had felt ignored by Washington for as long as they could remember found that their votes really could change things – whether to the astonishment, dismay, trepidation or delight of every-one else.

My polling and political commentary over the years amount to a prolonged re-minder that the voters are worth listening to. Sooner or later, they will make themselves heard. If the events of 2016 help to remind the powerful of those truths, that sounds to me like a good thing.

MAA

January 2017

1 / Donald Trump v. Hillary Clinton

"You have two devils. Which devil do you pick?"
(Hispanic focus group participant, Florida, October 2016)

PERHAPS THE MOST WIDELY QUOTED FACT about the 2016 election was that it was contested by the two least popular candidates in presidential history. Not surprisingly, Democrats were more or less content with the direction of the country after eight years of President Obama, and Republicans were most assuredly not. But the reasons for the historically low approval ratings for both contestants went well beyond the deep and bitter partisan divide which had become a depressingly familiar feature of American politics over many years. Certainly, Donald Trump and Hillary Clinton both had their upsides and their fervent supporters. But for huge numbers of voters, both had failings that made the choice the most unpalatable they could remember. For many, including registered supporters of both parties, the question became which combination of flaws and virtues rendered their holder the least unsuited to the presidency – which of them was, in the phrase we heard night after night in our focus groups in swing states, "the lesser of two evils."

Often, people expressed bemusement that in a country the size of America, the choice should have come down to this. "I feel like I'm in *The Truman Show*," a young, Republican-leaning dairy farmer told us in Wisconsin. "I can't fathom the fact that we got here as a nation, where my choices are what I consider to be terrible and ridiculously terrible." An undecided woman in Pennsylvania summed up the daily struggle throughout the campaign to settle on an answer: "I think 'I can't vote for her', so I go, OK, I'm going to vote for Donald Trump, and then every time he opens his mouth I go 'good God!'"

Having taken the Republican primaries by storm, Trump clearly had an appeal among the GOP base which was, we found, shared more widely among voters unhappy with the way things were going. The attraction was simple: at a time when many had given up on politicians taking them seriously or getting anything done on their behalf, he was the very embodiment of change. For a start, he was not a politician and did not try to behave like one: "He doesn't say stuff just because you want to hear it. He says what he feels and what he thinks," one Midwestern Republican explained in defence of his decision to vote for Trump in spite of his reservations. It is hard to overstate how refreshing many voters found this quality after, as they saw it, a stream of politicians forever trimming and hedging and trying to ingratiate themselves with all sides.

Trump was, above all, a businessman, and this brought with it two further appealing attributes: a practical approach to solving problems, and the independence that comes from great wealth. His success as an entrepreneur proved he knew how to cut deals and make things happen – another bracing departure from the politics they knew. When it was revealed early in October that in 1995 Trump had declared a loss of $916 million – meaning he may not have paid any income tax for eighteen years – the news barely dented his appeal. Indeed, we found that for those tempted to vote for him, it served as further evidence of his business prowess and common sense. "He's smart," declared a woman in Virginia. "Who wants to pay more taxes than they have to? My husband works for himself. I take every deduction I can take. I'm not paying extra taxes."

And his personal fortune (more often a hindrance for candidates, especially on the centre-right) meant he was not beholden to donors, special interests, party apparatchiks, or anybody else: "He's not a politician and I don't feel he's in bed with everyone else in Washington," a Trump supporter told us in Virginia. If he needed to blow up the system, there would be no constraints: his priority would be "looking after the American people."

Crucially, Trump seemed ready to act on the things voters cared about. People in our focus groups worried about jobs, healthcare costs, crime, prospects for their children, the welfare system, immigration, the impact of trade deals and America's place in the world, and these were the issues on the Republican candidate's agenda. This agenda – and, even more importantly, the way he articulated it – also heralded the welcome end of what many saw as a left-liberal drift in policy and an ever more politically correct culture. Nobody expected him to solve every problem, but he would change course: "He's not going to do everything in four years, or eight years, because they've made such a mess," one of his supporters told us in Virginia. "But I think it will go in the right direction, point us in the right direction and get something done." For conservatives, the clinching argument for holding their nose and voting for Trump was often the Supreme Court: "Supreme Court justices are appointed for life. So if she gets in and appoints three or four justices, the Supreme Court will be turned in a liberal direction." This alone was reason enough to tolerate this flaws.

If the specifics of his programme were otherwise opaque, this mattered little to voters who were attracted to his broader priorities and message of change. After all, politicians made promises all the time, to no obvious effect. "Politicians say how they're going to fix everything, but they never do it. So what's the point? You say what you're going to do but you never do it," as a Trump-leaning Wisconsin voter put it. Neither did they much mind about his lack of political experience: "Being a businessman he's not a stranger to asking for advice," and "he's smart enough, even if he's not as smart as he thinks he is, to put the right people in the right place."

Politically, the potential downsides of a Trump presidency were the corollary of his virtues. Would the willingness to say exactly what he thought, which made him such a compelling candidate, make him a liability in diplomatic relations? "I think there are enough protections in place, enough laws in place, and there's just enough power that's offset from the president that if Trump wins I don't think it could go super-super south on a domestic stage," an undecided voter in North Carolina told us. "But on an international stage, with his brashness, you know, insulting people, I'm not sure how well we would be doing a decade from now." And as we heard from a young voter in Wisconsin, among many others: "I feel like he's a loose cannon, he doesn't have any kind of filter, he just says whatever, and it's not necessarily a good thing when you're dealing with other countries and global conflict." When we asked our groups what was the worst that could happen with Trump in the White House, the answer was very often "World War Three."

While some found his tone bracingly forthright, for others it was hurtful and divisive, especially on the question of immigration. One Hispanic woman in Phoenix told us, "I've been raised in Arizona, I've been here fifty-four years, I don't know a lick of Spanish, and it just bothers me that his first attack was, 'we're going to get rid of all the criminals, we're going to build this great big huge wall'. Everybody wants to keep the drugs out, the cartel, the people that are coming here illegally, we want them to be here when they're supposed to be – but just the way he first came out and started talking about it, it wasn't a good feeling for me." Another agreed: "I think he's brought up a lot of bad American feelings towards immigrants, and that's what really bothers me." (It should also be noted, though, that the Hispanic voters we spoke to were by no means universally hostile to Trump, or his stance on immigration. The rules needed to be enforced, they often argued: their families had had to go through the proper process, and a lack of control was unfair on aspiring immigrants from countries which did not happen to share a border with the United States.)

On a personal level, too, some of Trump's flaws were the flipside of his strengths. Where people applauded his outspokenness, his supporters often winced when this tipped over into causing offence, apparently deliberately. "He can't keep his mouth shut, he can't act presidential," complained one of our participants in Pennsylvania. "I like the things that Trump is bringing forth, but at some point there's got to be professionalism, there's got to be honour, integrity, and he's just lacking in them." "He appealed to me, and I love the guy," added another, "but then he goes too far and starts acting like a fifth grader. He just doesn't know when to pull back." And another in Virginia: "I'll be sitting there listening to him, thinking 'yes, yes, yes, oh why did you say that?'"

The Republican nominee's string of (to put it as neutrally as possible) provocative remarks reached their culmination after Hillary Clinton used the first presidential debate to mention Alicia Machado, a former Miss Universe whom Trump had apparently taunted about her weight and called "Miss Piggy" and "Miss Housekeeping." Trump responded with a series of tweets in the early hours of the morning in which he described Machado as "disgusting" and declared that Clinton had been set up by "a con." The following week, a tape was leaked of a private conversation between Trump and Billy Bush, presenter of *Access Hollywood*, which had taken place in 2005. Listeners were treated to a lewd description of Trump's approach to women who caught his eye – descriptions which, as his detractors pointed out at length, amounted to boasting about sexual assault. In the days that followed, a number of women claimed that these boasts were by no means empty.

For some voters who already disliked Trump, these events were another good reason to keep him out of the White House. As a woman in Ohio, despairing of the choice before her, told us the week before the election: "I can't stand behind someone who says the things he says. If I wouldn't want my daughter to marry someone like that, or to look up to someone like that, or my son, then I don't want to vote them in the presidency. In good conscience I can't vote for either, because I disagree with Hillary on some policy issues and some other things, and I disagree with Trump's character."

But the episode was not the game changer that many assumed it would be. As we found in our groups, his supporters did not simply dismiss these stories – they weighed them in the balance and decided that other things mattered more. "I wish he was a different man, but he's not," a man in Pennsylvania told us sadly. "But I don't want another career politician. I want change, and Trump is going to bring change." And a supporter in Arizona: "I don't condone it, but I'm looking at our country and what our country needs, and the issues." Some also pointed out that the outrage unleashed by Trump's supposed attitude to women had been absent in other cases: "I think about the Kennedys and their escapades, and it was fine with everyone because it was the Kennedys. They swept it under the rug, Kennedy after Kennedy after Kennedy. Then all of a sudden we have Trump, and it's like, 'oh my gosh, hide the children!'"

On paper, Hillary Clinton's strengths as a candidate could have been designed to exploit Trump's shortcomings. If he was new to the game, she had experience to spare. If he was temperamental, she was measured. If he was hazy on policy issues, she was always well-prepared, fluent and articulate. For some of the undecided voters we encountered, this was enough. "I don't trust any of the politicians, honestly," a man with a military background told us in Florida. "But given her experience, she has less chance of starting World War Three, because she has the international political connections." And a woman in Ohio, who was struggling to make up her mind days before the election: "You have to pick the person who at least knows something about the country. If I pick Hillary it will be because she's been in politics thirty years and Donald Trump don't know nothing about the politics of America." Indeed, for some, the mere fact that she was not her opponent was sufficient: "There's just no dignity to him at all, nothing respectable. He's not the type of president we want, we don't want him representing our country," as a man in Virginia, no great fan of Clinton, told us in October.

Even among Democrats, these reasons for choosing Clinton hardly amounted to enthusiasm for their candidate, and certainly did not match the fervent desire for change among supporters of her opponent, whatever his flaws. Asked how they would feel if she won, their most common reaction was "relief" that he would have been kept out of office.

As with Trump, the downsides of Clinton were the flipsides of her strengths. Her experience was the result of her decades in politics, which made her the ultimate Washington insider – the personification of the political establishment that so many longed to be rid of. Moreover, said her opponents, this experience was actually "bad experience", if you examined her record. Her decisions as Secretary of State, they argued, contributed to the deaths of Americans in Benghazi – which, for her many critics, put Trump's misdemeanours neatly in perspective: "Hillary didn't send air support to keep those four guys alive but they're worried about Trump saying mean things to women. I think that's completely ridiculous", as one of his Virginia supporters put it.

Perhaps even more damaging in electoral terms, Clinton's long "experience" made it impossible for her to respond convincingly to the demand for change that was driving support for Trump in the places she needed to win. "She's been a politician in this country for longer than I've been alive," a young woman in North Carolina observed, "and now she wants to talk about doing all these things, and it's like, lady, you've been in office this long, you know, and that's something I realised last night watching the debate." At best, a Clinton presidency would mean no change; at worst, it would mean going further in the wrong direction.

By the same token, if Clinton was measured, prepared, fluent and articulate, this also made her scripted and insincere. A politician, in other words. For many voters, the televised debates that were supposed to show the almost embarrassing gulf between the two candidates' preparedness for office showed something else. As a man in Virginia told us after the first duel, "He's up there showing who Trump is. She's up there showing who that polished politician is, and then going behind the curtain and being her true self there."

But this distrust was more than a matter of taking a politician's words with a pinch of salt. People in our groups regularly told us they thought Clinton was shady, corrupt or worse. There was a feeling that with the Clintons you never quite got to the truth, and that their first instinct was to cover things up. A trivial but damaging example occurred two months before the election, when Hillary Clinton collapsed briefly at a 9/11 memorial ceremony in New York. Having initially stated that she "felt overheated", her campaign later announced that she had been suffering from pneumonia. People felt that this opacity also surround the Clintons' financial dealings, especially when it came to the Clinton Foundation and the suggestion that its donors had been given special access to her as Secretary of State.

The suspicion that the Clintons were reluctant to be transparent about things – combined with old stories like the suicide of Vince Foster, an adviser in Bill Clinton's White House – led many people to assume the worst and to believe the outlandish conspiracy theories promoted by anti-Clinton commentators on talk radio and online. In our first two nights of focus groups participants told us that Hillary Clinton had had people killed, that she talks to the dead, that she had had affairs, that she had advanced Parkinson's and that one of her bodyguards was really her neurologist.

Only a small minority believed such things (albeit a bigger minority than we had expected). But even among voters not inclined to accept the wilder accusations there was a feeling that Clinton played by different rules from everyone else. This, rather than the potential national security implications, was for voters the most telling aspect of the revelation that she had used a private email server as Secretary of State. Many times, focus group participants who had worked in junior or mid-ranking positions in government offices or the military told us that they could have expected to be fired or even prosecuted for doing what she did. At the very least, as an independent voter in Arizona put it, she just has "bad judgment. Whether it's the email server or the Clinton Foundation, I don't know if it's criminal, but it's just bad."

For many voters, Clinton's pattern of behaviour pointed to a sense of entitlement. "I always picture her as someone who thinks it's her turn, and it bothers me," one man told us in Wisconsin. "Whenever I see her going to Hollywood and earning all that money, and speeches on Wall Street, it just seems like she thinks it's *her turn*."

If, then, people felt they had to decide which candidate was the least unsuited to the presidency, why did enough people in enough places conclude that Donald Trump's flaws were the more forgivable? As ever, the answer lies not with the candidates but the people choosing between them. Trump's failings were personal, but (provided he appointed good advisers, as people expected, and managed to control his temper at the G8 Summit) had no real bearing on the way he ran the country. Clinton's were also personal, but they were metaphors for bigger things – things that affected the voters. Many of the voters who tipped the scale thought Trump an uncouth billionaire with an unedifying attitude to women, but for them Clinton represented business as usual, and a Washington clan that lived by different rules, ignored the people they were supposed to represent and had no plans to improve their lives.

This, it turns out, was the bigger disqualification from office.

2 / Brexit part II?

"There is something eerily familiar about some of the themes from our first week of research. Many people want a new direction, and seem prepared to accept the risks that they know go with it. Those who want change appear more motivated than those who would rather keep the status quo. And it is hard to see what new information will help people decide between the two. Now, where have we heard that before?"
(First *Ashcroft In America* focus group report – Green Bay, Wisconsin, 23 September 2016)

DONALD TRUMP LIKED TO SAY during his campaign that the 2016 presidential election would be "beyond Brexit", "Brexit plus", even "Brexit times ten." He meant that as with Britain's EU referendum earlier in the year, the result would defy the pundits, and he was right about that. But he was right in other ways too. I immodestly opened this chapter with a quote from my own work to highlight just how striking the similarity was to an outsider who had spent two years watching how voters approached their decision on the other side of the Atlantic.

The parallels are not exact. Since American voters were choosing an individual, in some ways they had a better idea of what they were getting than their British counterparts: Donald Trump in the White House, the Oval Office, the Situation Room. Moreover, they were selecting a leader, not changing the way their country was governed;

indeed, we found that the limits of presidential power were a comforting thought for many of his more reluctant voters. And while Trump would be president for four years with the option to renew, Brexit was for life (and beyond). But there were similarities between Trump and Brexit went beyond anti-establishment sentiment and an unexpected result.

The change and the risk

Many British voters who wanted to leave the European Union tended to think life was getting worse for people like them, were unhappy with the level of immigration and the impact they thought it was having on the economy, public services, and the character of their society, and thought they had more to lose than to gain if things continued as they were.

In the weeks leading up to the presidential election, American voters drawn to Donald Trump spoke in much the same vein. They complained about a welfare system that promoted entitlement but punished work; lax immigration controls that threatened national security, jobs, and the American way of life; the worries they had for their children's future in a changing economy; the high and growing cost of health insurance that many of them faced; and their continual struggle to maintain a good standard of living for their families ("the new American dream is to survive rather than thrive, to make it through," as one woman told us in Green Bay). They feared the erosion of constitutional freedoms and saw a mushrooming culture of political correctness which, far from promoting civility, was creating and entrenching division. And they believed the United States was losing its status in the world: "Iran shoots over the top of our ships and we don't do anything about it," said a man in Cincinnati. "No-one takes us seriously anymore." It was time to "end all the apologising" in foreign affairs.

For British Leave voters, remaining in the EU did not just mean sticking with an unsatisfactory status quo. It meant carrying on a process. This had started harmlessly enough forty years previously when the UK joined the nine-nation Common Market, as it was popularly known, but had reached a point where the citizens of twenty-seven countries had the automatic right to live and work in Britain, and European law had primacy in many areas of policy and legislation. With more countries set to join and plans for deeper integration afoot, staying did not mean keeping things as they were but continuing down a path which many thought had already gone too far.

In one sense, Hillary Clinton represented business as usual: the insider's insider, the embodiment of the American political establishment. But by continuing the leftward drift that many thought had brought America to what many saw as its parlous current state, she too would represent something worse than the status quo. As these voters saw it, policy under her presidency would continue to go in the wrong direction, with further damaging consequences for themselves, their families and the country at large – and by bringing about a liberal majority on the Supreme Court, she could entrench these unwelcome changes for a generation or more.

Brexit meant change, and so did Trump. But exactly what kind of change, no-one could be sure. Change therefore meant risk. For many in Britain, the big downside of leaving was uncertainty: would we be able to do as much trade with the EU? Would our influence in the world grow or shrink? Would there be more jobs or fewer? Would we have more clout when negotiating with China and the US, or less? The absence of "facts" to guide their decision was a constant frustration for confused voters. Yet a month before the referendum, my research found that one in four of those leaning towards a vote for

Brexit were doing so even though they thought leaving the EU was a bigger risk than staying. Three quarters of those leaning towards a Leave vote thought "the importance of controlling our own affairs" was a bigger consideration than "the risks to the UK if we make the wrong decision." Ultimately, people decided that that UK was strong enough to prosper independently, that they were prepared to take an economic hit as the price of taking back control, or that things were already so bad that they had nothing to lose.

Across the Atlantic, the risks of Donald Trump were rather better defined. Since most regarded his policy positions as opaque at best, the promise of change came not so much from what he would do as who he was: an outsider, someone different, a non-politician who would come to Washington and shake things up. Accordingly it was Trump's character and temperament, rather than his plans, that constituted the biggest risk. Some of his pronouncements on the campaign trail may have been refreshingly candid, but "I don't know that I want him going into diplomatic relations." Did we want a Commander in Chief who "just flies off the handle"? Or to have to worry lest the new president "runs that yap and gets us in World War Three"?

Many also worried about what they saw as Trump's personal behaviour: the language he used about immigrants (which they feared could deepen divisions, even if they agreed that tougher immigration policies were needed), or his predilection for personal insults, or in the way he talked about – and, allegedly, treated – women.

As we saw in the previous chapter, it would be wrong to conclude that Trump's voters ignored these things, or dismissed them. They did not: they simply weighed them in the balance and decided there were other, bigger things at stake. Like the British voters who were prepared to live with the uncertainties that came with Brexit, Trump voters decided to take the risk of putting their man in the White House. The downsides of Trump had to be set against the "potential for a bigger reward." For a man in Ohio, it came down to this: "We know we're not going to get any change with Hillary… A lot of people feel like, let's roll the dice, and we're going to have to put up with a whole bunch of bad stuff, but maybe we'll get some things done with Trump."

Surprise!

The fact that so many Americans made this calculation came as more of a shock than it should have done to many close observers of the political process. This echoed the astonishment of much of the British political and media world which had failed, five months earlier, to understand that reasonable people might vote for Brexit. There was an assumption in certain circles that anyone wishing to leave the EU must be stupid, ignorant, prejudiced or mad. The fact that many Remain supporters thought this was abundantly clear to those inclined to vote to Leave. Far from making them think twice, it galvanised them: it proved to them that large parts of the governing stratum of society not only failed to understand their concerns but actively looked down on them, thereby making them all the more determined to vote as they wished.

It also ignored the fact that large numbers of Leave voters did not fit the Remainers' stereotype of them. In my research[1] six months before the referendum, when segmenting the electorate according to their characteristics and attitudes we identified a group we called *Global Britain*: voters who tended to be educated, with professional jobs, optimistic both for themselves and the country, and with an outward-looking view of Britain's place in the world.

---

[1]   *Leave To Remain: Public Opinion And The EU Referendum,* December 2015, LordAshcroftPolls.com

The notion that only a lunatic would vote for Brexit also led the Remain camp to overplay its hand. It warned of economic catastrophe, political instability and threats to national security, and even hinted at the prospect of war. Though they well understood that Brexit brought uncertainty and risk, voters thought these prophecies of doom became so overblown that they started to laugh them off, and began to dismiss even the most sober warnings as more "scaremongering", and ultimately, as the campaign dragged on and on, "white noise."

Something of the same phenomenon could be seen in America. Hillary Clinton's description of Trump supporters as "a basket of deplorables" didn't make any of them think twice: it merely sparked the creation of the "Proud To Be A Deplorable" T-shirt industry. Trump's critics held that his language and behaviour were outside the bounds of acceptable political debate and that he, and therefore his supporters, were beyond the pale. But this did not make any of his backers in our focus groups less determined to vote for him – only, perhaps, reluctant to admit their affiliation to friends and colleagues. Many who thought Trump's flaws disqualified him from office assumed that any reasonable person would think so too. But as we have already seen, this was not the case – not because his flaws did not matter, but because for many others the desire for change (and the determination to avoid a Hillary Clinton presidency) was so strong that they voted for him anyway.

As the day drew closer, the polls had Clinton ahead nationally, and in most key states. The assumption among most people in the political world was therefore that she would win, probably comfortably. But the polls were wrong, and therefore the pundits were wrong too.

Or so the story goes – and there is something in it. Of the last twenty-two polls conducted in Wisconsin, and the last nineteen in Michigan, not a single one put Trump ahead. But there is another explanation – that observers used the poll numbers to re-inforce what they expected to happen anyway, and were not as prepared as they should have been for the result that came to pass. As Sean Trende[2] set out on *Real Clear Politics*, the national polls actually performed better in 2016 than they did in 2012. But overall, the state polls performed exactly as well as they did four years ago. Battleground state polls in 2016 had a mean error of 2.7 points – exactly the same as in 2012 – but this time they favoured the Democrat rather than the Republican. As Trende concludes:

> What occurred wasn't a failure of the polls. As with Brexit, it was a failure of pun-ditry. Pundits saw Clinton with a 1.9 percent lead in Pennsylvania and assumed she would win. The correct interpretation was that, if Clinton's actual vote share were just one point lower and Trump's just one point higher, Trump would be tied or even a bit ahead.
>
> Instead, people gravitated toward unreliable approaches such as reading the tea leaves on early voting or putting faith in Big Blue Walls, while ignoring things like the high number of undecided voters. They selected these data points rather than other possible indicators, such as the significant late break in the generic ballot that could have led them in a different direction. To be blunt, people saw what they wanted to see, and then found the data to support that view.
>
> So don't blame the polls. They did what they were supposed to do, and in fact, did their job as well as they did in 2012. Instead, blame the analysts and pundits, and their stubborn resistance to considering the possibility of a Trump presidency.

2   *It Wasn't The Polls That Missed, It Was The Pundits*, Sean Trende, RealClearPolitics.com, 12 November 2016

A question of attitude

Please say which statement in each pair you most agree with, even if you don't completely agree with it. [Net]

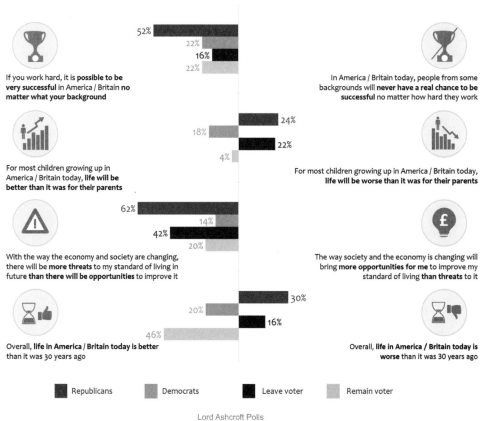

If you work hard, it is **possible to be very successful** in America / Britain **no matter what your background**

52%
22%
16%
22%

In America / Britain today, people from some backgrounds will **never have a real chance to be successful** no matter how hard they work

For most children growing up in America / Britain today, **life will be better than it was for their parents**

24%
18%
22%
4%

For most children growing up in America / Britain today, **life will be worse than it was for their parents**

With the way the economy and society are changing, there will be **more threats to my standard of living in future than there will be opportunities** to improve it

62%
14%
42%
20%

The way society and the economy is changing will bring **more opportunities for me** to improve my standard of living **than threats** to it

Overall, **life in America / Britain today is better** than it was 30 years ago

30%
20%
16%
46%

Overall, **life in America / Britain today is worse** than it was 30 years ago

■ Republicans   ■ Democrats   ■ Leave voter   ■ Remain voter

Lord Ashcroft Polls
🐦 @LordAshcroft

My thirty-thousand sample poll taken shortly before the presidential election revealed sharp differences between people of political outlooks that go beyond straightforwardly political questions. The differences between those identifying as Republicans and Democrats closely mirrored the split on similar questions between Leave and Remain voters in my post-referendum poll[3] in June 2016.

By a small margin, most Remainers thought that for children growing up in Britain today, life would be better than it was for their parents; Democrats thought the same about American children, by a somewhat bigger margin. Leavers and Republicans, meanwhile, thought life would be worse for children growing up in their respective countries. Most people in all groups felt that changes in the economy and society would bring more threats to their standard of living than opportunities to improve it – but Leavers and Republicans thought so by much bigger majorities than Remainers and Democrats. And while Remainers and (especially) Democrats thought that, overall, life was better in their country than it was thirty years ago, Leavers and (especially) Republicans believed the opposite.

Similar patterns were evident in their views of whether various ideas had proved a force for good or for ill. Democrats and Remainers took a more positive view of the Green movement, feminism, and (especially) immigration, multiculturalism and social liberalism than their opponents.

3   *How The United Kingdom Voted On Thursday… And Why*, 24 June 2016, LordAshcroftPolls.com

Do you think of each of the following as being a force for good, a force for ill, or a mixed-blessing? (10-0 scale)

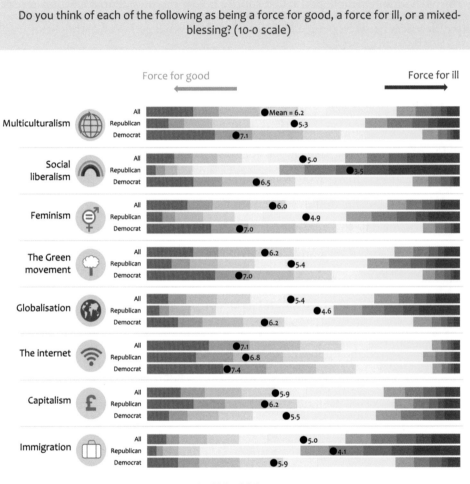

Force for good   Force for ill

Multiculturalism
All — Mean = 6.2
Republican — 5.3
Democrat — 7.1

Social liberalism
All — 5.0
Republican — 3.5
Democrat — 6.5

Feminism
All — 6.0
Republican — 4.9
Democrat — 7.0

The Green movement
All — 6.2
Republican — 5.4
Democrat — 7.0

Globalisation
All — 5.4
Republican — 4.6
Democrat — 6.2

The internet
All — 7.1
Republican — 6.8
Democrat — 7.4

Capitalism
All — 5.9
Republican — 6.2
Democrat — 5.5

Immigration
All — 5.0
Republican — 4.1
Democrat — 5.9

Lord Ashcroft Polls
@LordAshcroft

Do you think of each of the following as being a force for good, a force for ill, or a mixed-blessing? (10-0 scale)

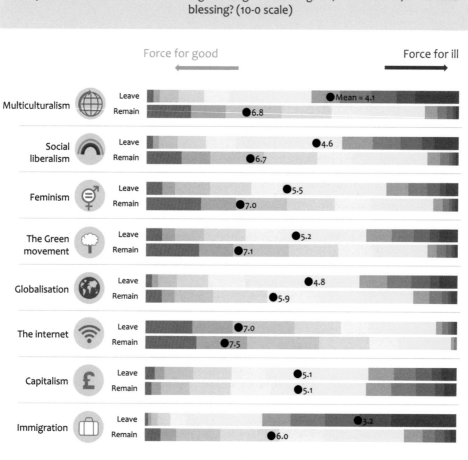

Force for good

Force for ill

		Leave	Remain
Multiculturalism	Leave	Mean = 4.1	
	Remain	6.8	
Social liberalism	Leave	4.6	
	Remain	6.7	
Feminism	Leave	5.5	
	Remain	7.0	
The Green movement	Leave	5.2	
	Remain	7.1	
Globalisation	Leave	4.8	
	Remain	5.9	
The internet	Leave	7.0	
	Remain	7.5	
Capitalism	Leave	5.1	
	Remain	5.1	
Immigration	Leave	3.2	
	Remain	6.0	

Lord Ashcroft Polls
@LordAshcroft

Globalisation hits home

In our poll, 44 per cent of Democrats said they thought globalisation had been a force for good. This compares to just 23 per cent of Republicans – including just one in five white Republicans, and only 14 per cent of Republicans aged 65 or over. In the UK, Leave and Remain referendum voters split the same way.

The slogan of the campaign for Britain to leave the European Union was "Vote Leave, Take Control." The idea that the country was losing (but could regain) the power to determine its own destiny was a powerful one for Brexit supporters. In my research[4] a month before the referendum, just over six in ten voters – including 85 per cent of those leaning towards a Leave vote – agreed that "we must have more control over our own affairs even if that means missing out on some of the benefits of co-operating with other countries"; only 39 per cent thought "we must be prepared to give away some control over our own affairs in return for getting the benefits of co-operating with other countries." When it came to comparing the two major competing themes in the EU campaign, just over half said "the risks to the UK if we make the wrong decision" weighed more heavily than "the importance of controlling our own affairs", but more than three quarters of those inclined to leave thought the latter was the bigger consideration. My post-referendum poll found that "the principle that decisions about the UK should be taken in the UK" was the single biggest reason Brexit supporters voted as they did – ahead of regaining control over immigration and borders.

Taking back control was also an important theme for many American voters. For them, too much power had been ceded not just to multinational bodies but to the

---

4   *Control v. Risk: Which Will Win Out In The Referendum Debate?* 26 May 2016, LordAshcroftPolls.com

global trade system, financial institutions, and a domestic political establishment that did not seem to share their priorities or values. Reactions to globalisation and its local effects were an important basis for Donald Trump's appeal. We have already seen that Republicans were more likely than Democrats to feel under threat from the way the economy was changing, and to see globalisation itself as a force for ill rather than good. In my pre-election poll we also asked specifically about trade deals, one of the main themes of Trump's attacks on recent administrations. While 41 per cent of Democrats thought that "in general, the US has benefited from free trade agreements with other countries", only 26 per cent of Republicans agreed. The great majority of GOP supporters thought America had "lost out" from such deals.

For some voters, the question of globalisation was about more than the impact of international trade deals on local industries and job prospects. Some feared that elements of the governing class, along with the Wall Street and business élite, were involved in a concerted effort to transfer power away from the US towards multilateral institutions. As one man put it in our North Carolina focus groups: "I don't think this election is about Republicans versus Democrats. What we are seeing is the globalists on both sides supporting Hillary against Trump, who is more for this country than a globalist. I think people are tired of the globalists. We saw that in the British exit vote a couple of months ago."

Now what?

One final parallel between Trump and Brexit: the question of what happens next. Nobody who voted to leave the EU knew for sure what that would entail, or what the consequences would be. As I found in my research on the new political landscape a few weeks after the referendum – by which time the country had a new Prime Minister as well as a new place in the international order – getting the right Brexit deal for Britain would be a good deal easier if only everyone would agree what the right deal looked like. Those who had voted to leave thought controlling immigration was more important than staying in the European single market, and those who had voted to remain thought the opposite. But to add to the pressure, many simply did not accept that any such trade-off existed. Why should we not continue to trade freely with our European neighbours while exempting ourselves from the free movement of people? At the time of writing the deal is a very long way from being finalised, but it is a good bet that someone is going to be disappointed.

The same may turn out to be true among those who backed the president-elect. In the days after the election the commentators asking each other what the Trump administration would look like and what it would do were not alone: his voters were doing it too. People who are worried by the outcome fear that the change will be too much. But there is also the hazard, as in Britain, that the change people want may not materialise in the form, or to the degree, that they feel they have been led to expect. Just as the details of Britain's trade relationship with Europe will have to be negotiated, Trump will have to come up against the barrier that some of his more reluctant supporters used to help justify their vote: the limits of presidential power. If, four years after gambling on Donald Trump, they judge that America is not being made sufficiently great again, what are they to do next? To quote one of our participants in Green Bay: "If he doesn't follow through, we'd be disappointed because who would we believe after that? We're just the peons in the world… I'd feel like, what's the point anymore?"

3 / The new American electorate

IN THE 2016 PRESIDENTIAL ELECTION, supporters of one candidate thought the other was a dangerous racist. Supporters of the other thought his opponent ought to be in jail.

But the divisions brought to the fore by the most polarised and polarising campaign in living memory go beyond people's reactions to Hillary Clinton and Donald Trump. We saw in the earlier chapter on comparisons between the November election and the Brexit referendum some of the differences in attitude between different kinds of voters that helped shaped both results. Republicans were more pessimistic than Democrats about prospects for children growing up in America relative to their parents, more apt to see threats rather than opportunities in the way the economy and society were changing, and much more likely to think life in the United States overall was worse today than it was thirty years ago. We also saw that Republicans were less inclined than Democrats to see immigration, multiculturalism, social liberalism, feminism and globalisation as forces for good. These point to some of the social, cultural and economic movements in America – and people's responses to them – have helped shape the divided political landscape that the scramble for the White House laid bare.

While these partisan divisions are real, the picture is more complex than that. Our pre-election poll asked thirty thousand Americans about not just their political views but a host of other things: their background, ethnicity, family, housing, education, health, work, income, interest in current affairs, religion, political commitment, where they get their news, their attitudes to big questions and their level of contentment with life. Ten distinct segments of voters emerge from our detailed analysis of the findings.

These, in turn, fall into four broad clusters: the Democrat Core, which provides that party with its most committed support; Centrist voters with no particular attachment to any one party; Republican Partisans who form the bedrock of the GOP; and what we have called Trump Targets – voters who have been less politically engaged but whose feeling that things had been going the wrong way in America made them fertile ground for Donald Trump's message and approach.

Within these clusters, our segments of voters have distinctive combinations of characteristics and attitudes which help to explain both the 2016 result and the state of American politics today, and have implications for the future. Plotted by their relative degrees of economic and cultural liberalism or conservatism, they look like this:

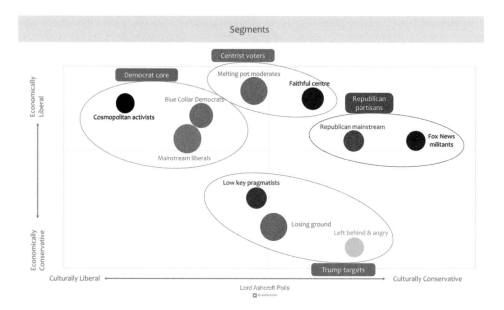

The Democrat Core
Mainstream Liberals: 15% of the population

This segment tends to be younger, female and highly educated, though racially similar to the US as a whole. Its members describe themselves as liberals or moderates, and have an average interest in politics. Local outlets, CNN and MSNBC are their most important sources of news. Just over half of *Mainstream Liberals* identify as Democrats, with a quarter describing themselves as Independents. People in this segment rarely attend church, and think that religion plays too great a role in political debate. They take an interpretive approach to the Constitution, and an overwhelming majority agree that it is more important to control gun ownership than it is to protect the right of Americans to own guns. More than two thirds of *Mainstream Liberals* think life in America is better than it was thirty years ago, compared to just under half the population as a whole. They are among the most likely to think of immigration and feminism as forces for good. Its members tend to be pro-choice, and overwhelmingly support same-sex marriage. They are more likely than most to think the US has benefited from free trade deals, to take a positive view of government regulation, and to favour investment in green energy.

59% say they always or nearly always vote; 77% say they always or usually vote Democratic

Blue Collar Democrats: 11% of the population

Members of the *Blue Collar Democrat* segment are the most likely to remain living in the town where they grew up. There is an even split between men and women, and its members tend to be younger, with a below average level of education. Half the segment is non-white, and one quarter is Hispanic. Half have children under eighteen, making them the group most likely to do so. The segment has an above average level of church attendance, and three quarters believe that religion is wrongly being driven out of American national life. One third identify as Catholics. They tend to be pro-life, and overwhelmingly support same-sex marriage. They are also among the most likely to see immigration as a force for good. Two thirds of this segment identify as Democrats or lean Democratic. Its members are moderately interested and active in politics, and are slightly more likely than most to name CNN as their most important news source. They are much more supportive of gun ownership rights than other parts of the Democratic Core. Members of this segment are more likely than most to see globalisation as a force for good, but also to think the US has lost out from free trade agreements with other countries. They are among the most likely to think the US should only defend itself and has no obligation to protect other countries, including NATO allies. They favour the idea of bigger government offering more services, and are among the least likely to think government benefits are too readily available. Though *Blue Collar Democrats* believe in climate change, they think protecting jobs and making today's energy more affordable is more important than investing in green energy for the future. They are more likely than average to think that life in America is better than it was thirty years ago, and that for most children growing up in America today, life will be better than it was for their parents.

61% say they always or nearly always vote; 67% say they always or usually vote Democratic

Cosmopolitan Activists: 7% of the population

Cosmopolitan Activists are the most active in politics, and are more likely to share political information on social media, attend rallies and donate to political campaigns than any other segment. They are disproportionately younger (with a quarter under the age of 24), female and in full-time education, though in terms of race the segment is similar to that of the US as a whole. They are the most likely of all the segments to possess a valid US passport. More than half say CNN is their most important source of news, but they are also more likely than most to name MSNBC (of the 37 per cent who say this, 59 per cent watch Rachel Maddow at least twice a week). An overwhelming majority of this segment identify as Democrats or lean Democratic, and three quarters describe themselves as liberal or progressive. They are the most likely to have a positive view of government regulation and benefits, gun control, investment in green energy, same-sex marriage, immigration, multiculturalism, social liberalism and feminism. They are very pro-choice and think religion plays too great a role in political debate. *Cosmopolitan Activists* are also the most likely to think globalisation has been a force for good and that the US has benefited from free trade deals with other countries (nearly two thirds agree with both propositions), and that the US has an obligation to defend its NATO allies. They are the least likely to believe it is possible to be successful in the US whatever your background, but more likely than most to think life will be better for most American children than it was for their parents. They are also among the most likely to think life is better in America than it was thirty years ago (four in five believe this to be the case), and to see opportunities rather than threats in the way society and the economy are changing.

77% say they always or nearly always vote; 92% say they always or usually vote Democratic

Centrist voters
Melting Pot Moderates: 14% of the population

Melting Pot Moderates are among the most likely to have been born outside the US, and nearly half the segment is non-white. Most see immigration and multiculturalism as mixed blessings, and they are more likely than most to be neutral or evenly divided on other questions, including gun control, the benefit of trade agreements and US intervention abroad. Nearly half describe themselves as moderate. Most lean Democratic, but they are the least likely to claim they vote at every election. This segment is positive about life in America today: they are among the most likely to think people who work hard can be successful in America whatever their background, and the most likely of all to think life is better in the US than it was thirty years ago and that American children today will have a better life than their parents. Most see more opportunities than threats from the way economy and society are changing.

57% say they always or nearly always vote; 62% say they always or usually vote Democratic

Faithful Centre: 9% of the population

Half of the *Faithful Centre* segment describe themselves as evangelical or born-again Christians. Church attendance is well above average, and three quarters of this group think religion is being wrongly driven out of American national life. Two thirds describe themselves as moderate or conservative, and there is an even split between Republican and Democrat identifiers. After their local news channel, they are equally likely to name CNN and Fox as their most important news sources. Members of this segment are the most likely of all to have been born outside the US; half of the segment is non-white, and a quarter are African-American. The *Faithful Centre* are divided on the benefits of immigration, gun control and trade agreements, but are strongly opposed to same-sex marriage and tend to be pro-life. They are more likely than most to see feminism and social liberalism as mixed blessings, but also to think that for most children growing up in America life will be better than it was for their parents.

59% say they always or nearly always vote; 48% say they always or usually vote Democratic

Republican Partisans
Republican Mainstream: 8% of the population

The *Republican Mainstream* group is disproportionately male, married, older, and has the highest white population (87 per cent) of any segment. More than nine out of ten identify or lean Republican, half describe themselves as conservative and a further quarter as moderate. They are more likely than most to have shared political information on social media, put up yard signs and contributed to political campaigns. Only one third describe themselves as born-again or evangelical Christians, but most think religion is wrongly being driven out of American national life. They tend to be pro-life and are more likely than most segments to be neutral or opposed to same-sex marriage. Of all the segments, the *Republican Mainstream* are the most likely to say that people who work hard can be successful in America whatever their background. However, they are also more likely than most to think that for most children growing up in America today life will be worse than it was for their parents, that changes in the economy and society are bringing more threats than opportunities, and that life in America is worse overall than it was thirty years ago. They are also among the most likely to think the US has lost out from free trade deals, that government benefits are too readily available, that social liberalism, globalisation and immigration have been a force for ill, and that feminism has been a mixed blessing. Just under two thirds say capitalism has been a force for good, making them the most likely to do so. They are also unusual in naming national security as their most important policy issue in their voting decision. *Republican Mainstream* members overwhelmingly say the Supreme Court should base its decisions on the Constitution as it was originally written and that protecting the Second Amendment is more important than gun control. Two-thirds name Fox News as their most important news source; of these, half watch *The O'Reilly Factor* at least twice a week. More than one third say talk radio is an important news source, making them among the most likely to say this.

76% always or nearly always vote; 88% always or usually vote Republican

Fox News Militants: 7% of the population

The *Fox News Militants* segment is predominantly white, Protestant and male. Of all the segments, its members are the most likely to be retired and to own their own home. Two-thirds identify as born-again Christians; they are the most likely to attend church at least once a week, and they strongly believe that religion is wrongly being driven out of American national life. They overwhelmingly identify as Republican and describe their views as conservative or very conservative, and are the most likely to put up yard signs. *Fox News Militants* are the most likely of all to be pro-life, Originalist, to support gun ownership rights, to oppose same-sex marriage, to favour smaller government, to think the US is the greatest country in the world, and to believe that people who have different views from them on politics have bad intentions for America, rather than simply misguided solutions. Though they overwhelmingly believe that people who work hard can be successful in America whatever their background, they are the most likely of all to think life for today's children will be worse than it was for their parents, and are nearly unanimous in feeling that the way society and the economy is changing brings more threats than opportunities. They are the most likely to think that life in America is worse overall than it was thirty years ago, and that multiculturalism, immigration, social liberalism, feminism, globalisation and the green movement have been forces for ill. *Fox News Militants* feel strongly that the US has lost out from free trade agreements, but two thirds think the country has an obligation to defend its NATO allies. They think regulation often imposes an unnecessary burden on business and that government benefits are too readily available, and are the least likely segment to believe that the earth's climate is changing because of human activity. They are the most likely to think that reporters who knowingly write false stories should face criminal charges and that Hillary Clinton should be in jail, and most think there is some truth in the idea that she is culpable for murder. Two thirds say Fox News Channel is their most important news source; of these, most watch *O'Reilly* at least twice a week and nearly half watch *Hannity*. This segment is also the most likely to say talk radio is an important source; of these two thirds listen to Rush Limbaugh at least twice a week.

79% always or nearly always vote; 90% always or usually vote Republican

Trump Targets
Low-Key Pragmatists: 8% of the population

The *Low-Key Pragmatists* segment is predominantly white and female. Most describe themselves as moderate or conservative, and two thirds identify or lean Republican. They have a below average level of church attendance, support same-sex marriage and are marginally pro-choice. Two-thirds think that life in America is worse today than it was thirty years ago, and they are more likely than most to think life will be worse for most children growing up in America today than it was for their parents. They are more likely than average to think immigration has been a force for ill. They tend to support gun ownership rights, are sceptical of bigger government, think the US has lost out from free trade agreements and are divided over whether the country has a responsibility to defend its NATO allies. Most name local outlets as the most important news source, followed by Fox News Channel and CNN.

59% always or nearly always vote; 61% always or usually vote Republican

Losing Ground: 14% of the population

Members of the *Losing Ground* segment are less likely than average to have a college education and are the most likely to be unemployed. Most describe themselves as moderate or conservative, and just over half identify or lean Republican, though they are less likely than most to take an interest in politics and among the least likely to claim they always vote. They are less likely than average to attend church. They are on the fence on some controversial issues but are more likely than most to see immigration as a mixed blessing or a force for ill. Members of the *Losing Ground* segment are among the most likely to think life in America is worse overall than it was thirty years ago, that the way society and the economy are changing is bringing more threats than opportunities, that life for most children growing up in America will be worse than it was for their parents, and that people from some backgrounds will never have a real chance to be successful no matter how hard they work.

49% always or nearly always vote; 55% always or usually vote Republican

Left Behind And Angry: 7% of the population

This segment is predominantly white, older, and less likely than average to have a college education. More than half describe themselves as conservative or very conservative, and most identify or lean Republican. The *Left Behind & Angry* segment has higher than average church attendance and its members think religion is wrongly being driven out of American national life. Most believe people who work hard can be successful in America whatever their background, though they are less likely than average to think this. However, most also think life will be worse for most children than it was for their parents, that life in America is worse overall than it was thirty years ago, and that changes in society and the economy are bringing more threats than opportunities. They are the most likely to think immigration has been a force for ill, tend to think the US has lost out from free trade deals, and are less likely than most to think America has a responsibility to defend its NATO allies.

59% say they always or nearly always vote; 64% always or usually vote Republican

*   *   *

It is worth exploring in more detail some of the differences in attitude that characterise the various parts of the American electorate.

Changing times

We asked in our poll whether people thought various changes in recent years had made America better or worse, on a scale where −5 meant "much worse" and +5 meant "much better." The mean result in each case suggested that people were fairly neutral about most of these. However, breaking out the results by party identification shows that a neutral overall score is not the same as a consensus.

Democrats think that more immigrants, same-sex marriage and gay adoption have made America better, while those who identify or lean Republican tend to think the opposite. But if we look at the ten segments in our model of the American electorate, we see that the divisions on such questions go much deeper than this.

Americans as a whole are quite closely divided as to whether "more immigrants coming to the United States" has made the country better (37 per cent) or worse (43 per cent). But within our Democrat Core cluster, more than nine out of ten *Cosmopolitan Activists* and *Blue Collar Democrats* say 'better"; meanwhile, more than eight in ten of the *Republican Mainstream* and *Fox News Militants*, and nineteen out of twenty of the *Left Behind & Angry*, say "worse."

Thinking about the following changes in America over recent years, do you think they have made America better or worse?

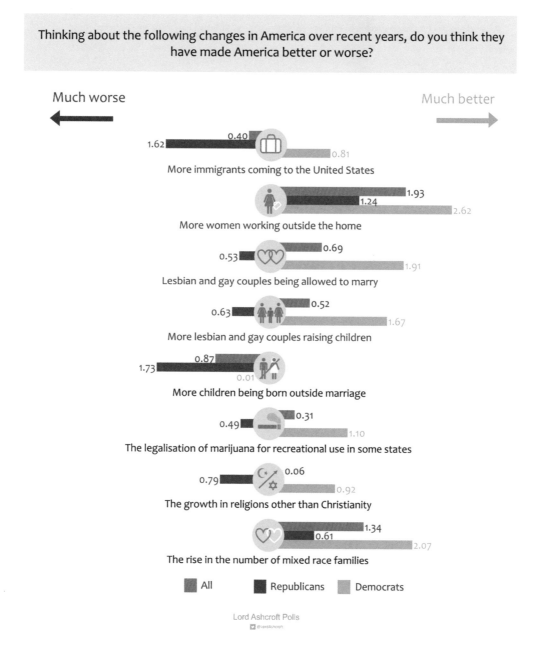

Much worse

Much better

More immigrants coming to the United States
1.62 — 0.40 — 0.81

More women working outside the home
1.93 — 1.24 — 2.62

Lesbian and gay couples being allowed to marry
0.53 — 0.69 — 1.91

More lesbian and gay couples raising children
0.63 — 0.52 — 1.67

More children being born outside marriage
1.73 — 0.87 — 0.01

The legalisation of marijuana for recreational use in some states
0.49 — 0.31 — 1.10

The growth in religions other than Christianity
0.79 — 0.06 — 0.92

The rise in the number of mixed race families
1.34 — 0.61 — 2.07

All   Republicans   Democrats

Lord Ashcroft Polls
@LordAshcroft

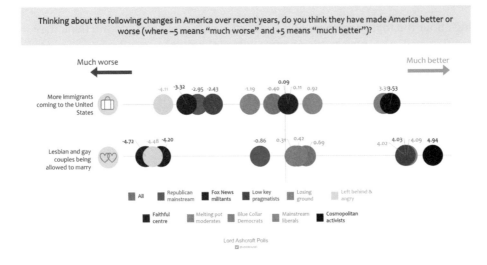

Thinking about the following changes in America over recent years, do you think they have made America better or worse (where –5 means "much worse" and +5 means "much better")?

Much worse

Much better

More immigrants coming to the United States

-4.11 -3.32 -2.95 -2.43   -1.19 -0.40 0.09 0.11 0.92   3.31 3.53

Lesbian and gay couples being allowed to marry

-4.72 -4.48 -4.20   -0.86 0.31 0.42 0.69   4.02 4.03 4.09 4.94

All	Republican mainstream	Fox News militants
	Low key pragmatists	Losing ground	Left behind & angry
Faithful centre	Melting pot moderates	Blue Collar Democrats	Mainstream liberals	Cosmopolitan activists

Lord Ashcroft Polls

The rift on same-sex marriage is even more stark. *Mainstream Liberals, Cosmopolitan Activists, Blue Collar Democrats* and *Low-Key Pragmatists* are all but unanimous in saying "lesbian and gay couples being allowed to marry" has made America better; *Fox News Militants*, the *Left Behind & Angry* and the generally moderate *Faithful Centre* almost universally disagree (but not, notably, the *Republican Mainstream*, who are largely neutral about the development).

Fears and priorities

Another way to understand the outlook and priorities of different kinds of voters is through the things they say they fear. In our poll we asked people to say how afraid they were that various things might happen – a score of zero meant they were not afraid at all, while a score of one hundred meant they were very afraid indeed.

On a scale of 0 (not afraid at all) to 100 (very afraid) please say how afraid you are that the following things may happen?

Not afraid at all ←   → Very afraid

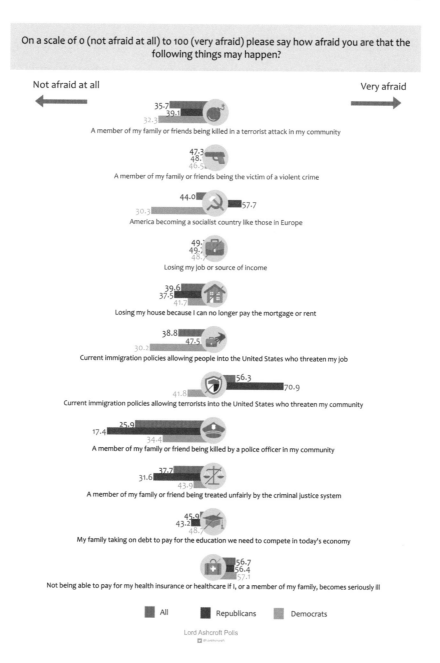

35.7
39.1
32.3
A member of my family or friends being killed in a terrorist attack in my community

47.3
48.
46.5
A member of my family or friends being the victim of a violent crime

44.0
57.7
30.3
America becoming a socialist country like those in Europe

49.
49.
48.
Losing my job or source of income

39.6
37.5
41.7
Losing my house because I can no longer pay the mortgage or rent

38.8
47.5
30.2
Current immigration policies allowing people into the United States who threaten my job

56.3
70.9
41.8
Current immigration policies allowing terrorists into the United States who threaten my community

25.9
17.4
34.4
A member of my family or friend being killed by a police officer in my community

37.7
31.6
43.9
A member of my family or friend being treated unfairly by the criminal justice system

45.9
43.2
48.
My family taking on debt to pay for the education we need to compete in today's economy

56.7
56.4
57.1
Not being able to pay for my health insurance or healthcare if I, or a member of my family, becomes seriously ill

■ All   ■ Republicans   ■ Democrats

Lord Ashcroft Polls
@LordAshcroft

Among our sample as whole, the biggest fear was "not being able to pay for my health insurance or healthcare if I, or a member of my family, becomes seriously ill." This featured in the top three of all ten of our segments. The second was "current immigration policies allowing terrorists into the United States who threaten my community" (a top-three concern among all groups except *Cosmopolitan Activists* and *Mainstream Liberals*) – ahead, even, of "losing my job or source of income" (which featured in the top three of just six of the ten segments).

Again, the figures show how anxiety about each event differs between Republican and Democrat identifiers, but looking at the different segments' responses is more revealing still. Two things are striking from these findings. The first is the various groups' overall levels of fear. The most anxious group of all is the *Blue Collar Democrats*. They seem to worry about nearly everything, giving fairly high and fairly similar mean scores to all eleven projected events, from 45.69 for "a member of my family or friend being killed in a terrorist attack in my community" to 60.42 for being unable to pay for healthcare. However, they are unusual in the Democrat Core cluster: *Mainstream Liberals* and *Cosmopolitan Activists* are much less fearful: the average score for the events overall was notably lower. Fear seems to be much more of a factor on the other side of the political spectrum. The Republican-leaning *Left Behind & Angry*, *Low Key Pragmatists* and *Losing Ground* segments, along with the partisan *Fox News Militants*, all profess high overall levels of anxiety.

The second thing worth noting is how afraid different kinds of voter say they are about different events. For four of the five Republican and Republican-leaning segments, the biggest single fear was "current immigration policies allowing terrorists into the United States who threaten my community" – a concern which barely registered with the *Cosmopolitan Activists*, whose biggest worries after healthcare costs were "my

On a scale of 0 (not afraid at all) to 100 (very afraid) please say how afraid you are that the following things may happen?

NB Top three fears

Cosmopolitan activists

	Being unable to pay for healthcare	57.32
	Taking on debt to pay for education	48.72
	Being treated unfairly by the criminal justice system	43.40

Faithful centre

	Being unable to pay for healthcare	54.14
	Immigration policy letting in terrorists	53.86
	Losing my job or income	45.18

Fox News militants

	Immigration policy letting in terrorists	88.09
	America becoming a socialist country	81.32
	Being unable to pay for healthcare	56.99

Losing ground

	Being unable to pay for healthcare	61.05
	Immigration policy letting in terrorists	60.61
	Losing my job or income	53.90

Lord Ashcroft Polls
@LordAshcroft

family taking on debt to pay for the education we need to compete in today's economy" and "a member of my family or friend being treated unfairly by the criminal justice system" (which in turn was low on the list for most right-leaning segments). For the *Republican Mainstream* and *Fox News Militants*, the second biggest concern was "America becoming a socialist country like those in Europe" – a prospect which made them more afraid, judging by the scores they gave, than any of the other groups were about being unable to pay for healthcare if they became seriously ill.

More about different voters' fears, and by extension their priorities for government, is revealed in our questions about climate change. Democrats are nearly twice as likely as Republicans to believe that the earth's climate is changing and that this "is mostly caused by humans doing things like burning fossil fuels"; GOP identifiers are more likely to think such changes "are mostly down to natural patterns in the earth's environment."

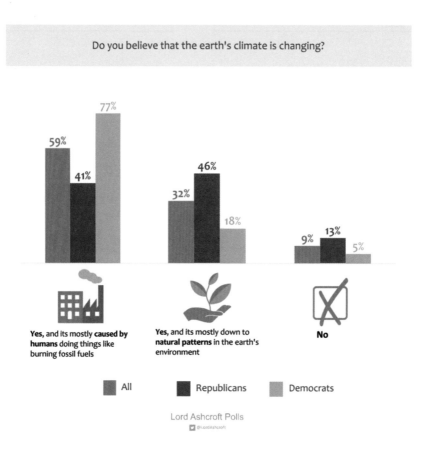

Do you believe that the earth's climate is changing?

Yes, and its mostly **caused by humans** doing things like burning fossil fuels

Yes, and its mostly **down to natural patterns** in the earth's environment

No

All   Republicans   Democrats

Lord Ashcroft Polls
@LordAshcroft

While 41 per cent of Republicans believe in climate change resulting from human activity, this falls as low as 22 per cent among the *Republican Mainstream* segment and just 14 per cent among *Fox News Militants*, one in four of whom do not believe the climate is changing at all. More than nine in ten *Cosmopolitan Activists* and 84 per cent of *Mainstream Liberals*, meanwhile, say climate change is caused by humans.

Accordingly, overwhelming majorities within the latter two segments say "we need to invest in the cleaner, greener energy of tomorrow even if it costs money and jobs in the short term," while *Republican Mainstream* and *Fox News Militants* (and, notably, *Blue Collar Democrats*) say "we should be protecting the energy jobs we already have and making today's energy more affordable" by similarly huge margins.

These divides are evident in practically all the areas of policy we looked in our poll. Asked to choose between two statements, nearly all the *Republican Mainstream* and *Fox News Militants* (and seven in ten *Blue Collar* Democrats) felt "it is more important to protect the right of Americans to own guns", while seven in ten *Mainstream Liberals* and 86 per cent of *Cosmopolitan Activists* thought "it is more important to control gun ownership." In a related question, huge majorities in those same Republican-leaning segments thought the US Supreme Court should base its decisions "on the Constitution as it was originally written", while 85 per cent of *Cosmopolitan Activists* and three quarters of *Mainstream Liberals* thought decisions should reflect the Court's "interpretation of what the Constitution means today."

Not surprisingly, Republican leaners and identifiers as a whole take a different view of bigger government, welfare benefits and state regulation than those on the Democratic side. Republicans are also more likely to believe that the United States has lost out overall from free trade deals with other countries, but views are less clear cut when it comes to American military intervention abroad. Clear majorities among the *Mainstream Liberals*, *Cosmopolitan Activists*, *Republican Mainstream* and *Fox News Militants* segments say that "as the most powerful nation in the world, the US has an obligation to defend its allies like NATO members, Israel and South Korea." In the more economically pressed groups – *Blue Collar Democrats*, *Losing Ground* and *Left Behind & Angry* – majorities say the US "should only defend itself" and has no such broader obligation.

Questions of race

Another set of divisions brought to the fore in the months leading up to the election concerned race. Our poll shed light on some of the differences in opinion between different groups – and revealed that on a number of important measures, African American and Hispanic voters are a good deal more positive and optimistic than their white counterparts.

Six in ten black respondents agreed that "overall, life in America is better than it was thirty years ago" – making them more likely to think this than whites (43 per cent), or indeed any other demographic group. And while the same proportion of African Americans also agreed that the way society and the economy were changing would bring "more threats to my standard of living than opportunities to improve it", this again made them less pessimistic on this front than the population in general (69 per cent), or white respondents in particular (71 per cent). Fewer than half of white respondents (44 per cent) thought that "for most children growing up in America today, life will be better than it was for their parents", compared to 58 per cent of Hispanic or Latino respondents and 61 per cent of African Americans.

Please say which statement in each pair you most agree with, even if you don't completely agree with it. [Net]

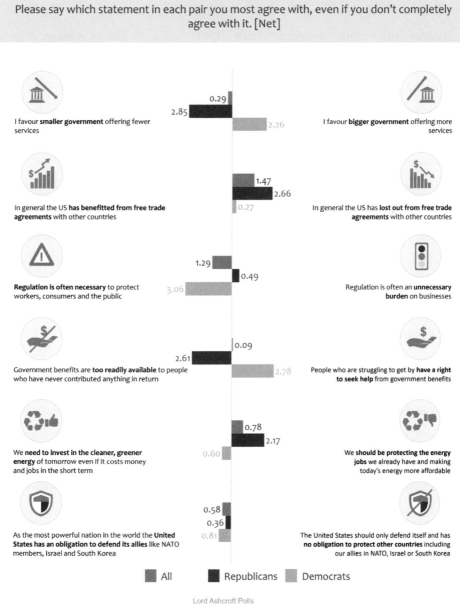

I favour **smaller government** offering fewer services

0.29
2.85
2.26

I favour **bigger government** offering more services

In general the US **has benefitted from free trade agreements** with other countries

1.47
2.66
0.27

In general the US has **lost out from free trade agreements** with other countries

Regulation is often necessary to protect workers, consumers and the public

1.29
0.49
3.06

Regulation is often an **unnecessary burden** on businesses

Government benefits are **too readily available** to people who have never contributed anything in return

0.09
2.61
2.78

People who are struggling to get by **have a right to seek help** from government benefits

We **need to invest in the cleaner, greener energy** of tomorrow even if it costs money and jobs in the short term

0.78
2.17
0.60

We **should be protecting the energy jobs** we already have and making today's energy more affordable

As the most powerful nation in the world the **United States has an obligation to defend its allies** like NATO members, Israel and South Korea

0.58
0.36
0.81

The United States should only defend itself and has **no obligation to protect other countries** including our allies in NATO, Israel or South Korea

■ All   ■ Republicans   ■ Democrats

However, this pattern was reversed on another question, which might be said to measure belief in the American dream. Only just over half of African Americans agreed that "if you work hard, it is possible to be very successful in America no matter what your background"; 43 per cent thought that "in America today, people from some backgrounds will never have a real chance to be successful no matter how hard they work" – higher than any other group by ethnicity, age, gender or level of education.

The answer to a further question helps explain this discrepancy. Our poll asked people how much they agreed that "African Americans and minorities have the same rights and are treated in the same way in the United States as whites", where zero meant the statement was completely false and a score of one hundred meant it was completely true. White respondents gave a mean score of 57.80, with two out of five giving a number above seventy. Two thirds of *Republican Mainstream* and *Fox News Militants* did the same, amounting to a mean score of 71 for both segments.

African Americans themselves, however, were much less likely to agree. Their mean score was just 27.9; more than half gave a number between zero and ten, the very bottom end of the agreement scale. Only one in ten gave a number between 91 and 100, indicating strong agreement – less than half the proportion of white participants who did so.

Comparing the fears of African Americans to those of the population as a whole sheds further light on this question of equal treatment. Black voters were no more or less afraid than the population as a whole of being unable to pay for healthcare, losing a job or source of income, current immigration policies letting people into the US who threaten their job, or family or friends being killed in a terrorist attack. But when it came to their fear of "a member of my family or friend being treated unfairly by the

Please respond to the following questions on a scale of 0 (completely false) to 100 (completely true) depending on the degree of truth you think is contained in each of the following statements.

"African Americans and minorities have the same rights and are treated the same in the United States as Whites"

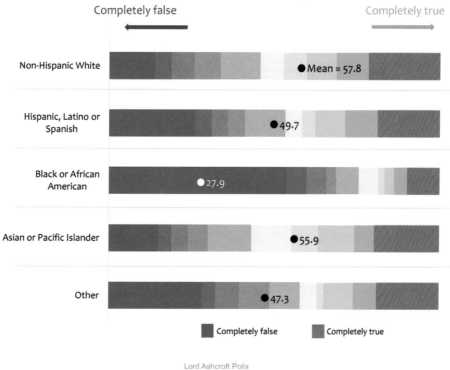

Lord Ashcroft Polls

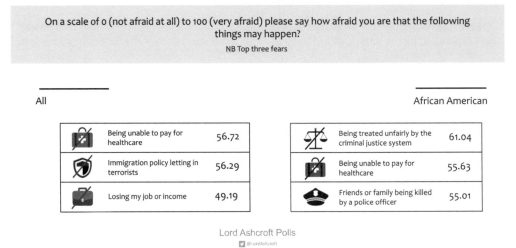

On a scale of 0 (not afraid at all) to 100 (very afraid) please say how afraid you are that the following things may happen?

NB Top three fears

All

	Being unable to pay for healthcare	56.72
	Immigration policy letting in terrorists	56.29
	Losing my job or income	49.19

African American

	Being treated unfairly by the criminal justice system	61.04
	Being unable to pay for healthcare	55.63
	Friends or family being killed by a police officer	55.01

Lord Ashcroft Polls
@LordAshcroft

criminal justice system", African Americans gave a mean score nearly twice as high as that of voters as a whole – making it the event they most feared of the eleven we tested. Their level of anxiety concerning "a member of my family or friend being killed by a police officer in my community" was also twice that of the general population, putting it third on their overall list of fears. (For respondents as a whole, these two events ranked ninth and eleventh respectively).

These issues were brought into sharp focus during the election campaign, when an African American man, Keith Scott, was shot dead by police in Charlotte, North Carolina. The shooting triggered protests, then riots, and the Governor declared a state of emergency. The following week, we held focus groups with African American voters in Raleigh, North Carolina's state capital. The Charlotte shooting had been the latest in a string of similar well-publicised incidents, but our participants did not think these were anything new – social media simply took them instantly to a global audience. As one young man said, "I grew up knowing that African Americans can just anonymously get killed from time to time. It's not something I'm OK with, but it's a fact of life." Intimidation of black people by the police felt routine: "I come from Prince George's County, and I've seen many guys just be stopped for no reason at all, and be harassed." Though many sympathised with the arguments of the law and order lobby, they first wanted to be sure that the law and order authorities would use their powers fairly: "We have to be able to trust that our police officers aren't going to target us or abuse this stop-and-frisk." And did they trust that? "No."

Part of the problem was that police officers rarely appeared to be disciplined after such events, and the authorities' instinct seemed to be to cover them up rather than get to the bottom of them. Moreover, little had changed on this front after eight years of President Obama. This suggested that the problem "has absolutely nothing to do with who's in charge, because there's an African American in charge and these things are still happening." After all, what could he do? "If I was a cop now and I went out and shot you, what's he going to do, call me on the house phone?… We have a black president now and this happened." This being the case, some felt, people were questioning whether it was worth showing up: "I feel like the recent events with policing have really discouraged a lot of black people from voting… 'If they're not even arresting people that are killing us, what does my vote really matter, does it really count?'" Few of these participants thought much had improved for them personally during the Obama years. He had shown people what they could achieve – "It inspires you to be better, 'there is a chance for me'" – but on a day-to-day basis, things are "still the way they are."

There was also a marked lack of enthusiasm for Hillary Clinton. "She just wants to be the first lady president. She wants to break history. She's kind of shady, though. She's kind of shady." Added to that, "I don't think too many people from the same family need to go to the White House. One is enough. They're trying to build a dynasty. They all really want power. Trump is a power fanatic, and Hillary Clinton, she wants power too."

But for these people, voting for her opponent was not on the cards. "His slogan, Make America Great Again, we want to get back America. Who are you going to get back America from? It's like he's going to put black people back to where they belong, where he thinks they belong;" "I don't think he's playing a card, I think he's being a direct bigot. He's attacking other people. This country was built on getting away from religious persecution and coming to a country where you could be free and you could be safe, and that's not what's going to happen;" "I think he wants to take us back to the fifties, before the Civil Rights Act, he wants to go back to dividing the colours, and I'd just be afraid."

From their point of view, Trump's campaign was about "exciting emotion. He can get the lowest emotion out of someone, and that's why he gets people elbowing people at these town hall meetings." They also feared there was a ready market for this kind of approach. "Another thing that makes this so dangerous is people feel like now they've had this black president they're ready to go back to what they know – which is all the other white guys, all the other fat white guys."

Enough already

One thing that unites the most committed voters on either side is the belief that those who disagree with them about politics must be less well informed than they are. Six in ten *Fox News Militants* and *Cosmopolitan Activists* think this, as do half of the *Republican*

Mainstream segment. (Endearingly, though, the *Blue Collar Democrats* are more likely to assume people they disagree with must be better informed than them than the reverse). Similarly, a majority of voters in nearly all groups (the exception again being the *Blue Collar Democrats*) consider that those who disagree with them must have different values from their own. Encouragingly, however, nearly four in five voters overall think that those who have different views on politics from their own "have good intentions but are misguided" (though four in ten *Fox News Militants* and more than one third of the *Left Behind & Angry* segment believe that such people "have evil intentions to change the United States").

All of which points to another finding from our focus groups, which gives at least some grounds for optimism: however strongly-held their views, people of all backgrounds and persuasions were painfully aware of the divisions in America, and regretted them. For our participants, these divisions had a number of causes – or, more accurately, the divisions that existed already were becoming deepened and entrenched.

For his critics, as we have seen, Donald Trump had a lot to answer for on this score. In the words of one of our Hispanic participants in Florida, his rhetoric had "tapped into something really down and dirty in our country." Some worried that children were copying some of the things they had heard him say, or felt he had given permission for people openly to express prejudices they would otherwise have kept to themselves: "Trump opened a closet where there were a lot of people who would not express some of their bigotry… Some people who were very quiet suddenly came out and said, 'oh, we can be ourselves'."

For others, including many who were no particular fans of Trump, the problem was not a resurgence of prejudice but a reaction to the creeping culture of political correctness which they saw as the real cause of division. Many felt that the emphasis on Barack

Obama as the first black president (and now on Hillary Clinton possibly becoming the first woman president) had heralded an era in which a person's race, gender and other personal characteristics had started to matter more, not less. The growing importance of identity was itself divisive: in the words of a non-partisan millennial in North Carolina, "People feel like they either have to side with the police or the Black Lives Matter movement."

Allied to this, people seemed ready or even eager to take exception to the most trifling things. As one Hispanic voter in Arizona put it, "We're so liberal, everyone's so quick to be offended by anything. I find Trump to be offensive but I kind of think we're at a point where we need a slap in the face. We've got to toughen up, and let's get back to being Americans and being normal people, and not being offended because the wind blew." Many felt that the liberal agenda had gone well beyond equality and the live-and-let-live attitude they were comfortable with to a point where they felt that they would be condemned for trying to defend their own values: "I feel like everyone has to be so politically correct these days, and I'm tired of it."

As well as their concerns for the direction of the country and relations between communities, there was another, closer-to-home reason why people wanted an end to the divisions (and could hardly wait for the election to be over): that politics was beginning to separate friends, colleagues and even families. Many said tensions were running so high that they had simply stopped discussing political questions at work, at home or on social media: tensions were running too high. In Ohio, one week before election day, a man who had reluctantly decided to vote for Trump told how disagreements had threatened to get out of hand: "Look at what's happened with Facebook. Everyone here is probably on Facebook, and you hate to get on it because someone's slamming someone else. One guy the other day: 'I've known you for fifty years', I went to kindergarten with him, 'how can you think that way, what is wrong with you?' I'm this close to de-friending him. Oh, fifty years of friendship because we disagree on a presidential election." The man realised there were more important things in life; the friendship lives on.

4 / News you can choose

WHEN WE ASKED WHAT WOULD EXPLAIN their candidate being defeated on 8 November, only one in five Republicans said the answer was simply that "another candidate has won fair and square in a tough but above-board election." Of the remainder, only one third said they would blame "a systematic effort by the authorities to rig the outcome." The biggest reason, according to a majority of GOP supporters – and two thirds of our *Republican Mainstream* and *Fox News Militants* voter types – would be that "the media has worked overtime to undermine the candidate you supported."

This distrust of the media was a recurring theme in our research, particularly among voters inclined to vote for Donald Trump. Participants in our focus groups complained that through selective reporting – omitting important details of stories, blowing others out of proportion, and ignoring still others altogether – the media presented, at best, a partial account of American politics, and one that certainly did not favour the right in general or Trump in particular.

For his opponents, the idea that the media were an obstacle to Trump's rise was laughable. At the Republican National Convention, the campaign manager of one his defeated primary rivals recalled how his team had been unable to persuade the TV networks to show up at a major campaign event for their candidate. But "if Donald Trump had farted on air, they would have covered it live, with a panel beforehand to discuss which way the wind was blowing."

If the candidate you're planning to vote for ends up losing the election for US President, which of the following will be the most likely reason for their defeat?

Another candidate has won fair and square in a tough but above-board election

35%
21%
49%

The **media has worked overtime to undermine** the candidate you supported

41%
54%
28%

There is a systematic effort by the authorities to **rig the outcome of the election** against your preferred candidate

24%
25%
23%

All   Republicans   Democrats

Lord Ashcroft Polls
@LordAshcroft

Be that as it may, Trump himself regularly denounced the media on Twitter and in his rallies, ultimately declaring in February 2016: "I'm going to open up our libel laws so that when they write purposely negative and horrible and false articles, we can sue them and win lots of money." He already had outlets in mind: "When the *New York Times* or the *Washington Post* writes a hit piece, we can sue them."

While some in the media worried about his attitude to free speech and a free press, his supporters had no such qualms. In our poll, nearly nine in ten *Fox News Militants* and *Republican Mainstream* voters agreed (giving a score of 70 or more on a 100-point scale) that "reporters who knowingly write false stories should face criminal penalties."

Perhaps ironically, the most fervent advocates of punishing false reporting were also the most likely to believe stories that have not been, shall we say, independently verified. Asked how much truth they ascribed to the statement "Hillary Clinton is culpable for murder," more than six in ten *Republican Mainstream* voters and three quarters of *Fox News Militants* gave a score of 70 or more out of 100 (a majority of the latter – 59 per cent – giving a score between 91 and 100). A majority of *Fox News Militants* think there is more truth than not to the contention that "there are cities in America where Muslims are instituting Sharia Law."

As we saw in the chapter on the new American electorate, different kinds of voters have pronounced differences in media consumption. More than two thirds of the two segments of Republican Partisans say Fox News Channel is an important source of news for them, compared to one in five *Mainstream Liberals* and only just over one in ten *Cosmopolitan Activists* (more than half of whom name CNN, compared to just eighteen per cent of *Fox News Militants*). Among those who listen to talk radio, more than six in ten *Cosmopolitan Activists* say they tune into NPR's *All Things Considered* at least twice a week, compared to just one in twenty *Fox News Militants* (two thirds of whom listen regularly to Rush Limbaugh; half say they listen twice or more a week to Sean Hannity).

On a scale of 0 (zero credibility) to 100 (absolute truth) how credible do you think each of the following controversial theories circulating on the internet is?

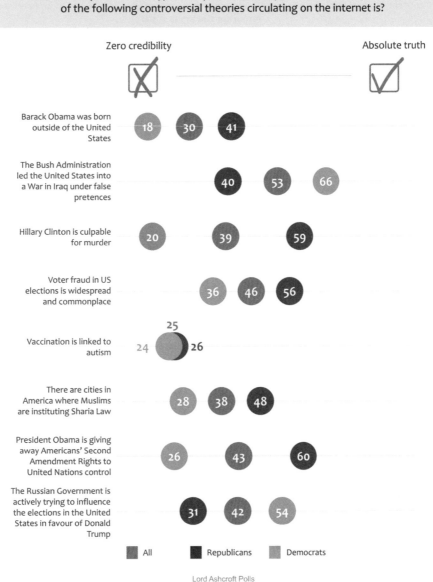

Zero credibility   Absolute truth

Barack Obama was born outside of the United States: 18, 30, 41

The Bush Administration led the United States into a War in Iraq under false pretences: 40, 53, 66

Hillary Clinton is culpable for murder: 20, 39, 59

Voter fraud in US elections is widespread and commonplace: 36, 46, 56

Vaccination is linked to autism: 24, 25, 26

There are cities in America where Muslims are instituting Sharia Law: 28, 38, 48

President Obama is giving away Americans' Second Amendment Rights to United Nations control: 26, 43, 60

The Russian Government is actively trying to influence the elections in the United States in favour of Donald Trump: 31, 42, 54

All   Republicans   Democrats

Lord Ashcroft Polls
@LordAshcroft

The following are some traditional media sources where people get news and information about politics. Please check any of the following that are important sources of information for you about news and issues facing our country or state.

NB Top three news sources

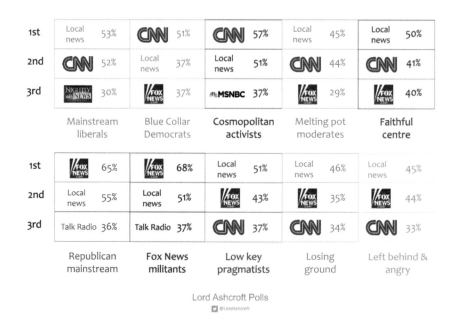

Lord Ashcroft Polls
@LordAshcroft

We can also see that for the Republican Partisan segments, right-leaning websites (sometimes labelled "Alt-Right", short for "Alternative Right") are an established part of the daily information loop. About one in five *Republican Mainstream* and *Fox News Militants* say *The Drudge Report* is "an important source of information for you about politics and news", and around one in seven name *Breitbart*, the news and opinion site previously run by Steve Bannon, Donald Trump's Chief Strategist.

Individuals who name Fox News Channel as an important source of information are considerably more likely than the population as a whole to believe that "Hillary

Clinton should be in jail for her crimes", that the Democrats would "attempt to steal the presidential election through election fraud", that "Hillary Clinton is culpable for murder", that "there are cities in America where Muslims are instituting Sharia Law" and that "President Obama is giving away America's Second Amendment Rights to United Nations control." (By the same token, *Cosmopolitan Activists*, who disproportionately get their news from CNN and MSNBC, are nearly twice as likely as the average voter to believe strongly that "the Bush administration led the United States into a war in Iraq under false pretences").

Observers regularly discuss (and usually lament) the influence of outlets that give a highly partisan outlook or report "news" that would not be found in most newspapers or on mainstream television channels. And as we found in our focus groups, voters who went to such sources ascribed a high degree of credibility to what they found there. But it is important not to get cause and effect the wrong way round. Someone may believe a dubious story because they hear it from a source they trust. But they are more likely to go to that source in the first place if they are open to the worldview it promotes and like the kind of stories it reports.

Another aspect of media influence that has been chewed over in this election cycle has been the role of Facebook (or "Fakebook" for those who worry about the spread of false news stories on social media). Our poll found just over a quarter of voters – including one in three in our Republican Partisan segments and nearly half of *Cosmopolitan Activists* – saying they had used Facebook to share political information. But we also found that Facebook sharers' mean likelihood of believing the controversial theories listed above was not significantly higher than for the population as a whole.

Even so, false stories are just as easy to share on social media as true ones, and whatever the relative degrees of cause and effect, people's ability to choose not just the views but the news that suits them is here to stay. So far, this development has given the Republican Party the most to contend with. For the prominent conservative talk radio host Charlie Sykes, who kindly gave us an interview for the *Ashcroft In America* podcast, the breakdown of traditional media has given rise to a "post-truth political environment." New outlets on radio and online, he argued, "have been so successful that we have created these alternative-reality silos where, if you're a conservative – it's true on the left as well – you can live in a world with your own facts, your own issues, and never encounter these fact-checks." We now had "the dark fever swamps of the right", which "traffic in the most bizarre conspiracy theories. And they're difficult to refute because too many conservative commentators do not want to challenge them. They know that their audiences will believe them." And just as you are tempted to dismiss a conspiracy theory as too far out of the mainstream, "Donald Trump, who may be the next president of the United States, is tweeting out links to these kinds of things."

In the Republican primaries and in the general election, the right-wing media, especially on radio and online, has been Trump's friend. But that was while he was an outsider pledged to "drain the swamp." We will see in the coming months and years whether, as President, he can hold onto the support of a media movement for which distrust of state authority is a guiding principle; how far Republican leaders in Congress and elsewhere feel they have to respond to an agenda promoted by a section of the media which, though narrow, commands the attention of a sizeable chunk of the party's base; and whether a similarly partisan or even "post-truth" media movement will make its presence felt on the left.

5 / **What happens next: the Democrats**

"I just don't know what her vision for the country is for the next four years. The status quo?"
(Focus group participant, Ohio, November 2016)

"'Vote shaming' Trump supporters is fair. What they have done is shameful."
(Op-ed headline, *The Guardian*, 19 November 2016)

LOSING POLITICAL MOVEMENTS tend to have one thing in common: the temptation to claim a moral victory. Parties that have been ejected from government like to comfort themselves with the notion that the electorate did not properly appreciate their achievements in office, failed to understand what was at stake, and had been bamboozled by a biased media. The voters, it follows, did not realise the horrors that lay in store for them under the incoming administration, and that they will come flooding back, full of repentance, as soon as they recognise their terrible error of judgment. A more extreme form of this condition is the belief that the voters have not merely been misled, but have deliberately behaved very badly indeed. Through base motives of greed or prejudice, they have rejected virtue and reason and knowingly chosen the dark side.

Both of these mindsets are evident in the way Donald Trump's opponents have responded to the election result. Some commentators and political professionals sigh that the working classes have voted against their own interests, especially when it comes to healthcare, and will be furious when this dawns on them. Others claim that voters were motivated by misogyny or racism (a curious charge, since the states that went over to Trump had elected and then re-elected Barack Obama). There have been calls for moderate Republicans to turn down jobs in the administration so as not to "normalise" Trump, as though not just the president-elect but his sixty million voters were a fringe movement outside the mainstream of acceptable political discourse.

For as long as the Democratic movement continues to interpret the election in this way, it can look forward to further defeats. As it should realise from its own history – not to mention those of both the main parties on my side of the Atlantic – the path back to power begins with a proper understanding of why you lost it in the first place.

When Americans were crying out for change, the candidate the Democrats offered was the very embodiment of the Washington establishment. When uncommitted voters in our focus groups talked about their worries – the cost of healthcare, their job security, prospects for their children, the effects of immigration, a seemingly unfair welfare system, or America's diminished place in the world – they had the sense that Donald Trump cared about these things too and would try to do something about them, even if his plans for doing so were not terribly specific. They expected no such change from Hillary Clinton, who as far as they could see represented a continuation of the policies that had either failed to deal with these problems, or indeed made them worse. If her experience made her in some ways a less risky candidate than Trump, for many people this was her only selling point, and a rather meagre one. As the official exit poll found, more voters wanted a candidate who "can bring needed change" than one "who has the right experience."

Perhaps sensing that it would always struggle to persuade people that Clinton had a new agenda for America, her campaign seemed to focus disproportionately on pointing out the flaws in her opponent. Her TV ads reminding voters that "our children are watching" and asking whether Trump was the kind of president they wanted for their daughters revealed much about the Democrats' approach: they themselves felt that no decent person could vote for Donald Trump – a candidate backed by a "basket of deplorables" – so all they needed to do was remind people of their moral responsibility to keep him out of office, regardless of any other consideration.

But for too many voters, other considerations mattered more than his personal failings. To the extent that those tempted by Trump associated Clinton and the Democrats with policy issues at all, it was with the burgeoning agenda of political correctness and identity politics which had reached its apotheosis in the fuss over transgender bathroom rights. The point was not so much that they disagreed with this agenda – though they did, fiercely – but that it had absolutely nothing to do with their own lives and the things they wanted their government to spend its energies on. Trump, not Clinton, was going to apply himself to the things they cared about.

Some Democrats take comfort from Clinton's margin in the popular vote (another branch of the moral victory argument). Yet the fact that she managed to rack up even more colossal totals than Obama in strongholds like California, New York, Massachusetts and Illinois while losing in Michigan, Pennsylvania and Wisconsin – famously failing to visit the latter even once after her defeat to Bernie Sanders in the state's

Democratic primary – illustrates the problem. The party pulled off the double whammy of taking crucial voters for granted while at the same time ignoring their concerns, or seeming to. That, in a nutshell, is what the Democrats have to face up to if they are to get back in the game.

Like the Republicans, the Democrats have a voting coalition that they need both to consolidate and expand. This task is made harder by two factors. First, they can no longer rely to the same extent on their traditional constituencies. Blue collar voters are one obvious example: exit polls found Trump trailing by just eight points among voters in union households, the narrowest margin since Reagan. Minorities are another. Black, Latino and Asian voters all supported Hillary Clinton by a smaller margin than that with which they helped elect Barack Obama.

My research suggests this is not just because they found her a less compelling candidate than the forty-third president. As an African American participant in one of our North Carolina focus groups said, "I can't believe that anyone would vote a straight ticket at this point. You've got to understand that all these people are really not working for you in any way – they just have a D or an R next to their name, and it doesn't really mean anything. The assumption that because they're Democratic means they're for black people, it's not true… Be an issue voter."

The second spanner in the works is that different elements of the existing coalition see things in rather different ways, and that these divisions could come to the fore as the party decides on its future direction. On the face of it, harmony reigns. The three segments from our research that make up the Core Democrat cluster of voters – *Mainstream Liberals, Cosmopolitan Activists* and *Blue Collar Democrats* – are happy about multiculturalism and same-sex marriage, are more optimistic than most voters that life for most children growing up in America will be better than it was for their parents, and named the economy, health care and education as the three most important issues when it came to choosing a presidential candidate. However, there is also clear potential for disagreement, and for some parts of the Democratic coalition to be alienated (or potential new voters to remain unconverted) if one strain of opinion becomes too dominant. In particular, we can see looming conflict between the highly educated *Cosmopolitan Activists* and the working class *Blue Collar Democrats*.

Cosmopolitan Activists are rather more sanguine about their own prospects in a changing world than their coalition counterparts. More than four in five of them think life in America has improved overall in the last thirty years, compared to just over half of *Blue Collar Democrats*. While two thirds of *Cosmopolitan Activists* think the way society and the economy are changing brings more opportunities to improve their standard of living than threats to it, most *Blue Collar Democrats* and *Mainstream Liberals* think the opposite.

Three quarters of *Cosmopolitan Activists* say they are liberal or progressive, but *Blue Collar Democrats* are much more likely to describe themselves as moderates. Not surprisingly, then, some important differences in values are evident. While 86 per cent of the former group say social liberalism is a force for good, only just over half of the latter agree; while 85 per cent of the former say religion "plays too great a role in our political debate", three quarters of the latter think religion "is wrongly being driven out of national life"; seven in ten *Blue Collar Democrats* say it is more important to protect Americans' right to own guns, while big majorities in the other two segments say it is more important to control gun ownership; and fewer than three in ten *Blue Collar Democrats* say abortion should be legal in all cases, compared to three quarters of *Mainstream Liberals* and more than nine out of ten *Cosmopolitan Activists*.

These differences also extend to the practicalities of policy. Two thirds of *Cosmopolitan*

Activists say the US has benefited overall from free trade deals with other countries, but two thirds of *Blue Collar Democrats* disagree. Big majorities of *Cosmopolitan Activists* and *Mainstream Liberals* think that "as the most powerful nation in the world, the US has an obligation to defend its allies like NATO members, Israel and South Korea", but most *Blue Collar Democrats* say the US "should only defend itself and has no obligation to protect other countries." And on energy policy, while most *Mainstream Liberals* and *Cosmopolitan Activists* think "we need to invest in the cleaner, greener energy of tomorrow even if it costs money and jobs in the short term", three quarters of the more hard-pressed *Blue Collar Democrats* think the priority should be "protecting the energy jobs we have and making today's energy more affordable" – even though, like others in the Democratic coalition, they also believe in climate change caused by the burning of fossil fuels.

The Democrats' success in negotiating these differences in outlook will determine their success in holding together their existing coalition of voters, and their ability to broaden it. Achieving the latter goal will also mean overcoming their disappointment and reaching out to voters with whom many in the party will feel they have little in common, or who have let them down by electing the wrong president.

The direction of the party will also depend on which of these groups has the ascendancy in the months and years to come. The *Blue Collar Democrats* are bigger in number and have more in common with the voters who handed Trump victory in the Midwest. But the *Cosmopolitan Activists* are the most likely to vote, to pay attention to politics, to share political information on Facebook, to talk about politics on Twitter, to forward emails to friends about candidates or issues, to attend rallies and, crucially, to donate money to political campaigns. They may be the smallest segment of the Democratic Core, but they are the noisiest.

The party has been here before. After Richard Nixon's victory in 1968, the Democrats chose a direction which led them from a defeat to a wipeout. Not for more than twenty years did they truly return to a commanding position on the centre ground, or the common ground, of politics. History, then, shows it is rarely wise for a party to allow its agenda to be set by an activist base whose values and agenda are most at odds with the people it needs to win over. We will see soon enough whether this is a mistake the Democrats are set to repeat.

6 / **What happens next: the Republicans**

"I want something new. I want the good old days back."
(Focus group participant, Ohio, November 2016)

IF SUCH A THING AS THE REPUBLICAN ESTABLISHMENT exists, it did not expect Donald Trump to become the party's nominee for president. Still less did it want this to happen. Current and former Senators, Governors, Congressmen, Cabinet Secretaries, White House advisers and others declared that he lacked the character, temperament, qualifications, principles or commitment to the Constitution required for the highest office in the land. Had he lost, the recriminations would have begun before sunrise on November 9: who was to blame for landing the voters with such a dreadful candidate and how could we ensure it never happened again?

In the event, the result gave rise to some unexpected and even more perplexing questions. First and foremost, who could take the credit (or, depending on your point of view, the blame) for his victory? To put it another way, did the Republicans regain the White House – and hold on to the House and the Senate – because of Trump, or in spite of him?

The evidence from our research suggests there is more truth in the former than the latter. In our poll, we compared people's levels of agreement with two separate statements: "The Republican Party understands the problems of people like me", and "Donald Trump is a Republican who I respect and support." In each of the Republican-leaning segments, Republican identifiers gave their level of support for Trump a higher score than their belief that the GOP is on their side (which was, even among these voters who considered themselves Republicans, little better than neutral). Trump, in other words, was more of a pull for them than the party – and the more partisan the segment, the truer this was.

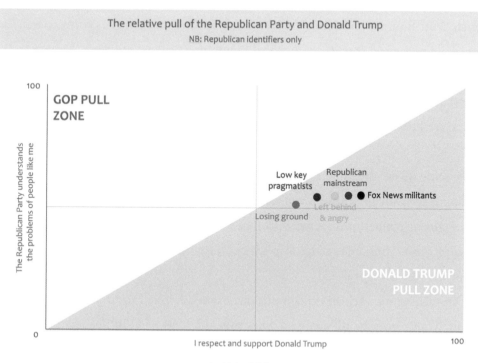

The relative pull of the Republican Party and Donald Trump
NB: Republican identifiers only

Our poll contained further sobering news for longstanding GOP leaders. Asked how much they respected and supported fifteen prominent individuals, Republican identifiers gave the highest ratings to Mike Pence, Ben Carson, George W. Bush and Donald Trump. The lowest mean scores were awarded to Mitch McConnell, Reince Priebus (though he may have risen in their estimations following his appointment as Trump's White House Chief of Staff), Carly Fiorina and Ted Cruz.

It is also instructive to isolate the responses of what we might consider the party's base. Republicans in the two most committedly partisan segments – *Republican Mainstream* and *Fox News Militants* – were more positive than Republican identifiers as a whole about everyone on the list except five: Paul Ryan, Mitch McConnell, John Kasich, Mitt Romney and John McCain. Most of the *Republican Mainstream* and *Fox News Militants* agreed that "Congressional Republican leaders care more about protecting the status quo than standing up for the principles of the Republican party"; only around one in three of them disagreed that "Republican leaders in Congress actually want to see Hillary Clinton defeat Donald Trump in the election."

By the same token, the more supportive the segment, the less likely its members were to think that "Donald Trump is typical of all Republican leaders." Small majorities in every segment tended to disagree with this statement (with the exception of *Cosmopolitan Activists*), but among the *Republican Mainstream* and *Fox News Militants* the proportion rose to eight in ten.

Our focus groups helped explain this dichotomy. As one Hispanic voter in Arizona told us, Trump may be different in tone from the kind of GOP leaders people had become used to, but "the stuff he says, the Republican party kind of brought it on itself. Climate change denial, I'm going to build a wall, lower taxes, the stuff that he

On a scale from -50 (Is a leader in the Republican Party I don't respect or support at all) to +50 (is a leader in the Republican Party whom I respect and support completely) how would you rate the following?

NB Republican identifiers only, all positions correct at time of fieldwork

is a leader in the Republican Party **I don't respect or support** at all

is a leader in the Republican whom **I respect and support** completely

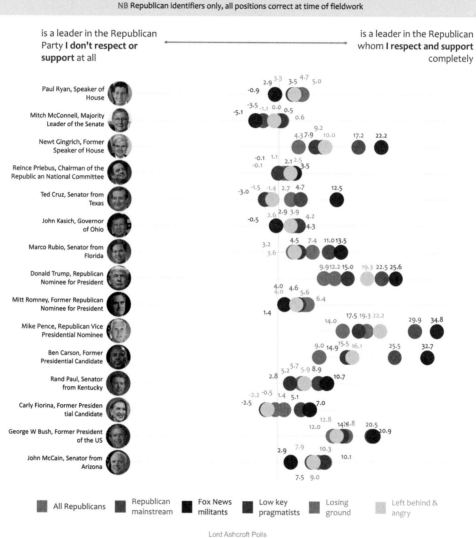

Paul Ryan, Speaker of House
-0.9 2.9 3.3 3.5 4.7 5.0

Mitch McConnell, Majority Leader of the Senate
-5.1 -3.5 -1.1 0.0 0.5 0.6

Newt Gingrich, Former Speaker of House
4.3 7.9 9.2 10.0 17.2 22.2

Reince Priebus, Chairman of the Republican National Committee
-0.1 -0.1 1.1 2.1 2.5 3.5

Ted Cruz, Senator from Texas
-3.0 -1.5 -1.4 2.7 4.7 12.5

John Kasich, Governor of Ohio
-0.5 2.6 2.9 3.9 4.2 4.3

Marco Rubio, Senator from Florida
3.2 3.6 4.5 7.4 11.0 13.5

Donald Trump, Republican Nominee for President
9.9 12.2 15.0 19.3 22.5 25.6

Mitt Romney, Former Republican Nominee for President
1.4 4.0 4.0 4.6 5.6 6.4

Mike Pence, Republican Vice Presidential Nominee
14.0 17.5 19.3 22.2 29.9 34.8

Ben Carson, Former Presidential Candidate
9.0 14.9 15.5 16.1 25.5 32.7

Rand Paul, Senator from Kentucky
2.8 5.2 5.7 5.9 8.9 10.7

Carly Fiorina, Former Presidential Candidate
-2.5 -2.2 -0.5 1.4 5.1 7.0

George W Bush, Former President of the US
12.0 12.8 14.1 14.8 20.5 20.9

John McCain, Senator from Arizona
2.9 7.5 7.9 9.0 10.3 10.1

All Republicans | Republican mainstream | Fox News militants | Low key pragmatists | Losing ground | Left behind & angry said during the primaries, they've been saying that for a long time… They have this big aura that they distance themselves from immigrants, they don't like immigrants from Mexico, or from pretty much anywhere."

For his strongest supporters, meanwhile, he represented a break away from the Washington establishment which, as far as they were concerned, included many of their party's own leaders. The distinction was sharpened by the refusal of some in the hierarchy to endorse Trump, and by the spate of denunciations and "un-endorsements" from senior Republicans that followed the release of the *Hollywood Live* tapes five weeks before the election. For many Trump voters these individuals had acted in a cowardly way, trying to distance themselves from a nominee they assumed was going to lose. They had "turned their backs on him", were "spineless" and "probably controlled by the donor class"; rather than acting out of principle as they claimed, this was "career politicians saving their ass so they don't ever have to work again."

All of this suggests that for all the agonising at the top of the party, despite the imperfections they saw in their candidate the "Never Trump" movement was always a minority pursuit among Republican voters. Most of them thought more highly of him than they did of the party, and its strongest supporters liked him most of all. Accepting this fact – if not necessarily enjoying it – is one prerequisite for a (relatively) harmonious future within the GOP in the years to come. Another is recognising that, like all election winners, Trump managed to win by assembling a coalition – and that, like all coalitions, this one harbours latent tensions that will need managing if it is to hold together.

As our poll suggests and the geographical pattern of his victory confirms, Trump won by mobilising the Republican base – represented in our segments by the *Republican Mainstream* and the *Fox News Militants* – while at the same time turning out large numbers of working class voters – our *Low Key Pragmatists, Losing Ground* and *Left Behind & Angry* segments – who are less likely to bother to vote, and who are less consistently Republican when they do.

There are several things that all parts of the coalition have in common, and which separate them from the other segments: the belief that life in America is worse today than it was thirty years ago, a strong likelihood of thinking that changes in the economy and society are bringing more threats than opportunities, and a belief that for most children growing up in America today, life will be worse than it was for their parents. Another is that of all the qualities that mattered to them in deciding how to vote for president, the one they mentioned most often was that they would "bring about needed change." (For *Mainstream Liberals, Melting Pot Moderates* and *Cosmopolitan Activists*, attribute that most often appeared in the top three was "clear ideas on the issues;" for *Blue Collar Democrats* and the *Faithful Centre*, it was that they were "honest and trustworthy.") But change comes in many forms, and the different parts of the Trump coalition see it in different ways. Both their priorities and their values overlap, but they are not identical and there are important differences in emphasis.

As we have seen, all five Republican-leaning segments say the terrorist threat from immigration and being unable to pay for healthcare in the event of serious illness are among their biggest fears. But while the *Republican Mainstream* and *Fox News Militants* fret about "America becoming a socialist country like those in Europe", those outside the base are more worried about losing their jobs. At the same time, all parts of the coalition do not share the same degree of hostility to immigration, or the same zeal for smaller government. Within the base segments, more than nine in ten say they favour "smaller government offering fewer services." *Losing Ground* and *Left Behind & Angry* voters are much more divided between this and "bigger government offering more services" – not least, perhaps, because more of them depend on these services themselves. They are similarly split, for what may be a similar reason, between the view that government benefits "are too readily available to people who have never contributed anything in return" or that "people who are struggling to get by have a right to seek help" from the state.

When it comes to questions of international relations, majorities in all the Republican-leaning segments think the US has in general lost out rather than benefited from free trade deals with other countries – a potential source of tension between the administration and the base on the one hand and a Congress more open to free trade on the other. But on potential military intervention around the world, different parts of the coalition have a different perspective. Most of the *Republican Mainstream* and two thirds of *Fox News Militants* think that "as the most powerful nation in the world, the United States has an obligation to defend its allies like NATO members, Israel and South Korea." Only just over one third of *Losing Ground* and *Left Behind & Angry* voters agree: majorities of both think the US "should only defend itself and has no obligation to protect other countries."

There are also some striking differences within the coalition on moral and cultural questions. While *Fox News Militants* and the *Left Behind & Angry* segment say all but unanimously that same-sex marriage has made America worse, *Republican Mainstream* and *Losing Ground* voters are much more ambivalent and *Low Key Pragmatists* almost universally think it has made America better. There is a similar pattern on the question of lesbian and gay couples raising children, and the *Losing Ground* and *Low Key Pragmatists* segments are very closely divided on the question of abortion. Nor do those outside the base share the near-unanimous preference of the *Republican Mainstream* and *Fox News Militants* for the protection of Second Amendment rights over controls on gun ownership.

Added to all this, the Republicans are now deprived of one of their most unifying and motivating forces of the 2016 campaign: Hillary Clinton. In our focus groups, in state after state, Republicans who found themselves wavering after Donald Trump's latest outburst or mishap would remind themselves of the alternative: "Some of the stuff he says just makes me cringe, but when you're looking at him compared to Hillary, those are my choices"; "He's a loose cannon and he has no filter, but at the same time, I know that one side is going to be an abject disaster"; "I don't know if he has the capability to be a good president at all. I just think he'll be slightly less awful than Hillary." Trump's next opponent is unlikely to have such a galvanising effect.

Consolidating the Republican coalition, then, will be a major political challenge for Trump over the next four years. But the party still needs to think about how to widen, as well as deepen, its support. Those who criticised the Trump strategy or doubted it could succeed said there were simply not enough angry white men in America to elect him. They have been confounded, though his appeal turned out to be broader than those critics suspected. Nevertheless, it would be a brave party that banked on being able to repeat its trick of winning the White House while losing the popular vote by nearly three million. As we have seen, Trump overwhelmingly won the support of Republicans, but we also know from our focus groups in swing states that many voters tempted to vote for change could not bring themselves to support the party in its current form, or this particular nominee. Such people will need to be brought into the fold if the party's winning coalition is to be sustained.

Our research points to two big clues as to the way forward. The first is for the different parts of the GOP leadership – whether in the White House, the Senate, the House of Representatives or the RNC – to recognise that they are, to coin a phrase, all in this together. After the most bruising campaign in living memory, relationships will inevitably be fractious. But as far as the voters are concerned, they now have a one-party government. With a president from one party and a Congress run by another there was an explanation (if not a particularly admirable one) for gridlock. Now there is no excuse not to get things done.

Here there is a chance for the Congressional leadership to redeem itself in the eyes of the GOP base, and with the public at large. There is a chicken-and-egg quality to the relatively low approval ratings for Speaker Ryan and Senator McConnell among Republican identifiers: does notoriously low satisfaction with Congress automatically carry over onto its leaders, or does dissatisfaction with their own performance transfer to the institution? Either way, they have a mission: to bring legislative coherence to the agenda on which Trump was elected, thereby showing that they – and Congress itself – are on the side of the people and have a constructive role to play. If Trump seems unable to get things done, history suggests he will not hesitate to blame Congress, and there will be a ready audience for that argument. Either all of them succeed, or none of them do.

The second point is that the change they enact must go with the grain of the voters' agenda, both inside and outside the Republican base. As the findings above show, there is not always a perfect coincidence between the two. *Republican Mainstream* voters and *Fox News Militants* want to see Hillary Clinton in jail and think reporters who knowingly write false stories should be locked up – but others in the coalition are not so sure, and in any case their priorities are closer to home. While there were plenty of complaints about the creeping effects of a liberal cultural agenda eroding people's rights and undermining their values, the plea was for this to stop – not for the culture wars to continue from the opposite direction. Protection of religious freedom and Second Amendment rights, together with a solid conservative on the Supreme Court, will show the base that they have been heard. Meanwhile, a focus on living standards, job security, healthcare costs, immigration reform, infrastructure, school reform, and a robust (but not too terrifying) approach to America's place in the world are potential ingredients for a programme to Make America Great Again that could amount to more than the sum of its parts. It could also reassure those who entrusted the Republicans with both branches of their government and tempt those who were too doubtful to make the switch this time.

Working with Congress to make this happen, and doing so in such a way as to satisfy the disparate parts of the Republican coalition, will inevitably mean compromise. This will be another big test for the new president. For his supporters, politicians are people who scratch each other's backs while selling out their principles and promises, but Donald Trump is a man who knows the art of the deal. Much depends on how well he can maintain the distinction.

Methodological note

Thirty-two focus groups were held between 20 September and 2 November 2016 in Green Bay, Wisconsin; Raleigh, North Carolina; Richmond, Virginia; Philadelphia, Pennsylvania; Phoenix, Arizona; Miami and Tampa, Florida; and Cincinnati, Ohio.

29,706 adults were interviewed online between 13 and 31 October 2016. Results were weighted to be representative of all adults in the United States. Full data tables can be found at LordAshcroftPolls.com

Charts and graphics in this publication have been produced with the help of The Noun Project.